LEAN
MOMMY

Lisa Druxman, MA

FOUNDER OF STROLLER STRIDES®

with Martica Heaner, MA, MEd

CENTER
STREET®
NEW YORK BOSTON NASHVILLE

LEAN
MOMMY

Bond with Your Baby
and Get Fit
with the
Stroller Strides®
Program

Neither this diet and exercise program nor any other diet and exercise program should be followed without first consulting a health care professional. If you have any special conditions requiring attention, you should consult with your health care professional regularly regarding possible modification of the program contained in this book.

Center Street
Hachette Book Group USA
237 Park Avenue
New York, NY 10017

Visit our Web site at www.centerstreet.com.

Center Street is a division of Hachette Book Group USA. The Center Street name and logo are trademarks of Hachette Book Group USA.

Printed in the United States of America

First Edition: June 2007
10 9 8 7 6 5 4 3 2 1

Library of Congress Cataloging-in-Publication Data
Druxman, Lisa.
    Lean mommy : bond with your baby and get fit with the Stroller Strides program / Lisa Druxman with Martica Heaner. — 1st ed.
       p. cm.
    ISBN-13: 978-1-931722-93-3
    ISBN-10: 1-931722-93-5
    1. Postnatal care.   2. Exercise for women.   3. Physical fitness for women.
I. Heaner, Martica K.   II. Title.
RG801.D78 2007
618.6—dc22   2006030714

DEDICATION

HOW CAN I dedicate this book to anyone but my children? It was Jacob who inspired me to start Stroller Strides. And it is both Jacob and Rachel who inspire me every day to be a better mom. I have learned the pureness of love and the joy of life from both of you. While my children were the ones who inspired me, it is my husband who supports me. Without you, Jason, I could not get through a day of what we have taken on. Without your blessing and support, there would be no Stroller Strides or any of these other wonderful projects. Every time I come up with a new idea, you encourage me to follow through. You are the wind beneath my wings! I dedicate this book to my family. I love you more than you'll ever know!

ACKNOWLEDGMENTS

FROM LISA

It is not often enough that we have the opportunity to thank those who help and support us each day. I am grateful for the opportunity to thank you all now.

Thank you to my co-author, Martica. This has been an unbelievable learning experience and I thought we made a great team. I hope you have learned and been as inspired as I have.

Thank you to my agent, Linda Konner, for believing in me and introducing me to such a great publisher. I do hope that this will be the first book of many that we create together.

Thank you to everyone at Hachette Book Group. Chris, you have been a joy to work with and we can't wait to share *Lean Mommy* with you now that you're a mom yourself.

And one thousand thanks to my Stroller Strides team. They didn't have a hand in writing this, but I could not have done it were they not doing such a fabulous job running my company. You are all amazing and I am so blessed to get to work with you each day.

I am blessed to have much support. Any mom knows the impossibility of getting things done with children around. I thank my Michael, Joel, and Bobbi for always helping with the kids so that I could finish this book.

And finally, this book is about how you as a parent can shape the future for your children. Thank you, Mom and Dad, for having such a positive impact on me. If you are proud of me, you should be proud of yourselves because I would not be who I am were it not for you.

FROM MARTICA

It is never easy to write a book. Much like having a baby, it's a process. I hope that Lisa and I have managed to give birth to not only an effective body-transforming plan, but a powerful way to help overcome the internal struggles that all women face.

I have come out of this experience with even more respect for Lisa than I had when we started. If anyone can be an inspiration to moms, it's she. Lisa is truly genuine and her passion is real. And she has an extremely wise head on her front-pack-strapped shoulders.

Thank you to Lisa, Linda Konner, Chris Park, Sarah Sper, and everyone at Hachette, and my friends and family. And even though he can't read, I thank my beloved sixteen-year-old cat, Fred, who purred on my lap during endless hours on my computer.

CONTENTS

A Mom, a Baby and a Mission

Motherhood. Welcome to the ultimate life-changing experience. As a new mom, no part of your life is recognizable, including your body, which is why you're now reading this book.

Being a mom can be the most wonderful and joyous time. But it's not always easy. Suddenly, on top of all your other normal obligations, you've got this new little one who trumps all other priorities! If you have a husband, other kids who still need your TLC, or another job among your responsibilities, it's no surprise that you feel overwhelmed, overworked, and, well, exhausted. And with society's focus on appearance, it's hard not to obsess on the physical aftermath of having a baby.

The one most likely to suffer from this scenario is you. If you're like most new mothers, you probably make yourself the last priority. Being a mom is all-encompassing. It's easy to become a martyr mom—giving up precious minutes for yourself, even though now is when you need me-time the most—not just to regain your pre-pregnancy shape, but to stay energized and healthy so that you can be the best mommy possible!

I'm a mom of two young kids. I've struggled through these pressures, too—and I continue to do so. As the owner of a national company and being a full-time mother, I find it extremely hard to practice what I preach. But on most days, I feel like I've mastered that juggling act. And through my company, Stroller Strides, I've helped tens of thousands of other struggling moms make it work, too. As a result, they look better and feel more confident than they ever have before (even before motherhood). You will read some of their inspiring testimonials throughout this book.

In the following pages, I will share with you the methods that have worked for Stroller Strides moms across the country. You'll see how becoming a Lean Mommy is not just a training of the body. It's a training of the mind. This book isn't about undertaking drastic dieting or boot-camp workouts to get back into shape. It's about getting more energy from food and exercise and overcoming the mental obstacles that block your ability to stay fit and make healthy choices. What's unique about this book is the focus on you being a positive role model for your family. If you don't do it, who will?

OVERCOMING OBSTACLES

We all know what we are supposed to eat, and that we are supposed to exercise. So why don't we do it? The secret tool to achieving the body you want is changing the way you think to develop a health-oriented perspective on your body. It's time to get off the diet cycle and start living a balanced life—if for no other reason than to teach your children healthy living.

I grew up in Southern California in a loving family. Yet, I remember from a young age feeling the pressure to achieve a better body. I spent my teens and early twenties going from one extreme diet to another and obsessing about exercising. I spent hours dissecting what I ate and even longer logging in workout sessions. When I would let up from my rigid patterns, I would binge. Despite my discipline, I never looked the way I wanted to. I was in shape, but I weighed thirty-five pounds more than I do today.

I gradually realized that the way I was living was not healthy, either physically or mentally. So I decided to release the constant pressure I put on myself. I took away all the food rules I lived by, and I started picking foods that would not only fuel me, but that would taste good and not leave me feeling deprived. I cut back on workouts and changed my motivation to exercise: I now exercised because I felt like moving, not to burn off as many calories as possible.

It worked. By relieving the anxiety I had felt toward exercise and eating, I became more at peace with myself. And by changing the behaviors that led to my unhealthy habits, the weight started coming off. It took time, conscious effort, and repeated attempts. But once I chose to live in a way that reaffirmed I wanted to be happy and fulfilled, rather than be a slave to what I looked like, my life improved dramatically. My personal training business became packed with clients when I started incorporating the same techniques that I used on myself. I created a program called L.E.A.N. (Learn Eating Awareness and Nutrition) to help other women achieve the same results. It was such a success that I began lecturing at international fitness conferences and renowned spas such as the Golden Door. *Lean Mommy* is based on this program.

> **OLD INSECURITIES RESURFACE**
>
> I make good eating choices to fuel my body. However, when we had to schedule photos for this book, that familiar pressure to diet and be thin re-emerged. I had not quite lost all of my baby weight. Yet I was supposed to show that it could be done! I snuck in a dieting attempt, but as soon as I did, I felt deprived and ended up making worse eating choices. Old habits die hard, including dieting habits. I realized that this was my chance to be a role model, not a bikini model. I am a happy, healthy mom in these pictures and you can be, too!

The key to my success was using a psychological technique known as cognitive behavior therapy. In a nutshell, you pinpoint the thoughts behind your unwanted behaviors, and then change the way you think to improve the way you act. People by human nature want to avoid pain and will do anything to achieve pleasure. This can manifest in different ways. For some, the constant effort of regular exercise and continually making healthier food choices is perceived to be tough, or painful. So they stick to what seems easy, or pleasurable: being a couch potato and eating anything and everything that is fast and tasty. Others may perceive being overweight as painful and thin as pleasurable. So they will go to any extreme to get there: crazy diets, over-exercise, and questionable treatments, drugs, or dietary supplements.

When I made my life-affirming switch, pain and pleasure were redefined for me. Following extreme behaviors and eating unhealthful foods now brought me pain. And feeling strong, energized, and good about myself gave me pleasure. So, dieting and deprivation were out; health and acceptance were in. Slowly, but purposefully, I changed the behaviors in my life that didn't contribute to my health. In *Lean Mommy*, you will learn how to live the lean life and also focus on your emotional well-being.

MY BEST LESSON IN HEALTH . . . PREGNANCY

Although my perceptions and priorities were now in the right place, it really wasn't until I became pregnant that I had my true "a ha!" moment. That's when I realized what real health was all about. From the start, I was in awe of my pregnancy. I took better care of myself than I ever had. I chose good foods because I wanted to fuel my baby's growth. I exercised because I knew it would benefit the baby, but I didn't overdo it because I wanted to protect the baby. Everything I did was for my child—deciding not to get my hair colored (because of the negative effect of the chemicals) or getting a massage because I thought the relaxation would be good for the baby. I got more sleep, stressed less at work, and never missed a day of vitamins. I took better care of myself during my pregnancy than any other time of my life. And I was at my happiest.

From the moment Jacob was born, I wanted to be the best mom I could be. I continued to stay nourished and fit to have the strength for everything that breastfeeding and motherhood demanded. It dawned on me later: What I did for myself then is what all of us should do and how all of us should think, all of the time, for the rest of our lives, not just during pregnancy. This wasn't only the birth of a new life, it was the birth of a new mentality. It had been years since I got off the diet roller coaster, but it wasn't until I became a mom that I can truly say that I embraced my own health. Sometimes, what we won't do for ourselves, we will do for our children.

As Jacob grew older, I found myself continuing to make better personal choices with him in mind. Whether it was not eating candy in front of him or making sure that our weekend activities incorporated activity, I was very cognizant of how my actions would shape his future—whether he would enjoy food and exercise, or struggle with them, and whether he would be able to make good choices. I realized that the only way that I could pave the way for a healthful existence for my children was to live and believe it myself and model the lifestyle that I wanted them to learn.

THE BIRTH OF STROLLER STRIDES

Finding my own balance inspired me to start a company to help other women do the same. During my pregnancy, I had been distraught at the thought of having to go back to work. But being a stay-at-home mom was just not an option for me. Once Jacob was born, my time with him became even more precious. I didn't want to drop him off at day care just so I could work out. But I needed to get back in shape: I was going to be offering a new weight management program for the line of clubs I worked for. It's a vain business I work in and I knew that I had to look fit to inspire others to do the same.

So I created a workout that I could do with Jacob. That hour together was the best for both of us. I discovered that

"IT took me thirty years and Lisa's help to gain control over my weight. Before I got pregnant I was 225 pounds. I had always been an emotional eater and tried diet after diet. Then I followed Lisa's L.E.A.N. and Stroller Strides' programs and finally found the motivation to stick to healthier habits long enough to see results and feel better about myself. I'm now 171 pounds and more than halfway to my goal. It may take another year, but I know that I will do it."

—JEN FRANKLIN, 35,
mom of Nicholas, 5, and Laura, 2,
San Diego, California

the stroller was a great tool for exercises like lunges and squats and the park could become a gym when I used tables for push-ups and benches for triceps dips. I had to make the workout baby-friendly. For instance, I quickly learned that I couldn't do cardio first and then plant Jacob in one spot for an extended time while I did my strength moves. There was no way that he would stay happy sitting still for too long. So I wove the two together, pausing to do a few strength exercises every few minutes during my stroller walk. Mom was happy. Baby was happy.

What I was still missing was socialization. I did not know a single other mom! Other moms must want to take off weight, I thought, and other moms must want to meet other moms. During a stroller walk with Jacob, I got the inspiration to start a playgroup-workout class in my neighborhood. Four people came to that first Stroller Strides class in Encinitas, California.

Word spread quickly, and one year later I had twelve locations and over 1,000 moms participating! Six years later, Stroller Strides has hundreds of locations and tens of thousands participating across the country. I share these details with you to show that I was not alone in wanting to get in shape, spend time with my baby, and feel better about myself—and neither are you. I now have two children. My daughter, Rachel, was about nine months old when we took these pictures for the book. With each of my children, I was able to get back to my pre-pregnancy weight in nine months simply with balanced eating and easy-to-fit-in Stroller Strides workouts.

"STROLLER Strides is the only workout I've stuck with and I don't feel guilty about leaving my son. I actually look forward to working out instead of dreading it."

—KELLY VAN JEN,
mom of Jason, 10, and Jessie, 5,
Vista, California

I'm here to help you look better, feel better, and to feel better about the way you look. If you follow my plan, I promise you will become what I call an Opti-Mom—a woman who is empowered to make life-affirming lifestyle choices.

An Opti-Mom trains herself to recognize that it feels good to live a healthy life, and that her body is meant to be loved and appreciated in the process. Her example conveys her positive mind-set and healthy behaviors to her kids. Our children learn from how we speak, act, and think. So by taking care of yourself, you are taking even better care of your children than you would as a martyr mom. Being an Opti-Mom allows you to focus on what *really* matters: your family. There should never be a moment that you miss in your baby's life because you are distracted, worrying about what you eat or a less-than-favorite body part. As an Opti-Mom who takes care of herself, you will get into the best shape of your life, and will become the healthy role model that your child needs.

Don't worry, I know that you want to share every precious moment with your new baby. The best thing about my program is that it won't take time away from your child, because your baby is with you every step of the way. *Lean Mommy* is the first book to help you bond with your baby while you work out. This way you can do what you need to do for yourself guilt-free—and baby will be giggling (or crying!) with you through every squat, lunge, and hill climb. Get ready to reach new levels of health, fitness, and inner peace.

CHAPTER 1

Your Post-Baby Body

You came out of pregnancy with a different body. Plus, the physical demands of motherhood take a real physical and mental toll. This chapter explains your new needs and how to emerge fitter and stronger than ever.

THE NEW YOU

During pregnancy, your body was a mixing pot of vastly changing hormones. Virtually every part of you was affected. There were profound changes in your cardiovascular system—including increases in the amount of blood that your heart pumped out and increases in your heart rate. A faster breathing rate helped you take in more oxygen and exhale the extra carbon dioxide that resulted from breathing for two. The amount of blood in your body increased and your body adapted to regulate its core temperature to keep baby in a favorable environment. Hormones like estrogen and progesterone increased. Your thyroid gland enlarged and your metabolism sped up, too.

As your baby grew, your anatomy changed. Your ligaments and

cartilage loosened because of the hormone relaxin. Your ribs, pelvis, and other joints expanded to accommodate your growing girth. Postural distortions and subsequent back pain may have occurred. Your balance may have been affected—and it may still be a little off as your body shifts back to being baby-less. Your feet, ankles, and knee alignment also may have altered to adapt to these postural changes.

Many of the hormonal adaptations that occur during pregnancy persist for months afterward. This period—from delivery to the point when the reproductive organs return to a nonpregnant state—is known as the postpartum period. The extra flexibility in your body may linger for up to three months, or even longer if you are breastfeeding. Extra mobility often means less stability. Some of these anatomical changes could last a lifetime if you do not take deliberate action to address them.

The new you is more fragile than you may think. You can't just jump back into the same old exercise routine (if you had one). And you shouldn't dive into a quick-fix diet. You have special needs now—unique physical, physiological, nutritional, and even emotional considerations that need to be factored into your new-mom life.

10 COMMON POST-PREGNANCY CHALLENGES

Being pregnant and delivering a baby are normal physiological states. But that doesn't mean that they don't wreak havoc on your body! Of course, with time, your body (mostly) reverts back to normal. But it's important to optimize the recovery process. And if you thought that pregnancy was tough on your body, you'll find out that the tasks of motherhood take their own unique tolls, too! But understanding the potential weaknesses in your postpartum body and doing what you can to strengthen them can help you alleviate or even avoid aches and pains. Here are common problems that new moms face—and how *Lean Mommy* will help you.

• POST-PREGNANCY CHALLENGE #1: POOR POSTURE •

Having twenty-five, thirty-five, or more pounds of baby weight in your belly created a shift in the way you held yourself. Your center of gravity moves forward as the baby grows and this often leads to an increased arch in your lower back, a rounded upper back, a forward tilt of your hip bones, and a slight jutting forward of your neck and head. Each woman's body adjusts differently, but everyone's body accommodates for the pregnancy. Worse, your muscles may strengthen to support this new way of holding yourself, and if you don't rebalance them, this distorted posture may stick with you for life.

WHAT YOU CAN DO ABOUT IT: Targeting the weaker, over-stretched muscles and stretching the tight, over-activated muscles can establish better muscle balance. Your body has become used to this alignment—both when the baby weight in your belly pulled you forward, and now when you hold him or her close or during everyday mommy duties like bending over while picking baby up, or getting the stroller in and out of the car. So, you may find yourself stuck in a constant forward slump all day. The *Lean Mommy* plan redresses this movement imbalance by integrating pulling motions to strengthen the muscles in the back to help you stand and move straighter and taller. Stretches for the tight pushing muscles in the chest also help keep you feeling upright rather than hunched. See pages 159–160, "Chest Stretch," and pages 132–133, "Tubing Row," for example.

• POST-PREGNANCY CHALLENGE #2: ACHING BACK •

It's no surprise that the posture distortion can strain your back. Even when you shed some weight, your back can still feel fatigued or painful because being a mom requires constant leaning forward and carrying extra weight. Bending over can be stressful for the spine because the discs between each spinal vertebra get compressed. When you're sleep-deprived, exhausted, and overwhelmed, you can forget to use the best posture to lift, carry, and hold your little one (and all his paraphernalia).

WHAT YOU CAN DO ABOUT IT: Learning how to minimize the load on your back during everyday mommy movements, such as when nursing or picking up baby, is the key to tackling neck, upper back, and shoulder pain. Plus, strengthening your core ab and back muscles to provide support when your spine needs it can help alleviate back discomfort. The *Lean Mommy* plan will show you how to make motherhood feel better simply by moving in a more effective way. You'll also learn ab and back moves to keep your torso strong and stable. See pages 59–62 and pages 117–118, "Baby Plank," and page 115, "Supermans," for example.

- **POST-PREGNANCY CHALLENGE #3:**
  ## TOO MUCH BELLY AND TOO MANY POUNDS •

The number one complaint of new moms is their tummy—a combination of lingering body fat, stretched-out skin, and poor muscle tone. Even if you didn't love your stomach before, in retrospect it looked much better than you ever realized! You wonder if it can ever feel flat or firm again. Some women eat more and become less active in the postpartum period and actually gain weight *after* they have the baby!

Women who are more active while pregnant are more likely to slim down after giving birth. But women who are active in the immediate postpartum period are also likely to drop a few dress sizes. Even though you should wait about six weeks before engaging in vigorous activity, there are things you can do immediately to incorporate exercise back into your life. Even if you've waited longer, it's never too late to start being active and reap the rewards. Although I'm not a proponent of worrying about your weight, it is important to get back down to a healthy weight because not doing so may contribute to *staying* overweight or even becoming obese in the future.

WHAT YOU CAN DO ABOUT IT: Your stomach will naturally recede as you lose your baby weight. The inches and pounds will come

"EXCITING news! I have an ab! Woo hoo! I might be getting another one soon, but Lisa is the one that has helped me get there. She rocks!"

—JEN COX, 38,

mom of Mackenzie, 5, Kelsey, 3, and Crosby, 18 months, San Diego, California off from staying active and making smart eating choices. But doing the right amount of physical activity and performing specific tummy-tightening moves correctly will ensure that you slim down and firm up in a way that's easy, safe for your joints, and more likely to be permanent. See pages 101–104, for example.

"IT took me a solid nine months to lose it, but now I am twenty pounds lighter than even before I was pregnant, and lighter than I was when I got married. Plus, I have the energy of teenager! (Good, I need it now!)"

—RACHEL PUSTILNIK, 32,
mom of Morgan, 3,
Richmond, Virginia

- **POST-PREGNANCY CHALLENGE #4:**
  UNCONTROLLED PEEING OR LEAKING •

When you were pregnant, the added weight and internal shifting of your organs magnified the pressure on your bladder, resulting in an increased urge to pee. If you had a vaginal delivery, you may have suffered trauma to the pelvic floor muscles, which can contribute to further incontinence. Either way you can end up with a permanently weakened bladder mechanism and pelvic floor muscles. You might experience just occasional leakage when you exert yourself (such as picking up the stroller, sneezing, or coughing). Or you may be silently suffering with a constant urge to urinate (even when there is nothing there), or a loss of control (you don't make it to the toilet in time). It's imperative to take corrective measures *now* because whether you experience incontinence later in life is associated with the level and length of time you experience incontinence after each birth.

WHAT YOU CAN DO ABOUT IT: Muscle fibers in the pelvic floor have an amazing recuperative ability. But you need to give them the proper stimulus. Most women can return to normal by performing pelvic floor exercises, as shown in the *Lean Mommy* plan. See pages 62–65.

- **POST-PREGNANCY CHALLENGE #5:**
  SEPARATED AB MUSCLES •

After your second trimester you may have noticed a gap at the midsection of your belly. This condition, known as diastasis recti, is a separation of connective tissue in your outermost abdominal muscle, the rectus abdominis. Because your ab muscles split and widen, the muscles provide less stability. There are varying degrees of separation and the problem can persist or even worsen if you're not careful.

WHAT YOU CAN DO ABOUT IT: You'll need to learn how to do corrective exercises to help the muscle fibers rejoin. The *Lean Mommy* plan helps you identify if you have this condition and shows ab exercises that will help. See pages 57–58.

- **POST-PREGNANCY CHALLENGE #6:**
  SCRUNCHED SHOULDERS •

I call it "the hunchback of motherhood": muscles that raise the shoulders tighten while muscles that hold them down weaken. Many mommy motions encourage this shoulder slump: bearing the weight of milk-heavy breasts, nursing baby, holding baby close, and carrying diaper bags, car seats, and strollers. If the back muscle that runs from your neck to your shoulders and upper back, the trapezius, spasms from being continually tight, you may feel neck strain or pain that can extend through your shoulders, back, and even arms.

WHAT YOU CAN DO ABOUT IT: Practice holding yourself in an upright posture, strengthening the back muscles while stretching the chest muscles. Learning to recognize—and stop yourself—when you slump is key. So, instead of bending over to breastfeed, you should bring baby up to your breast. The *Lean Mommy* plan includes exercises to help you hold yourself erect and to train the back muscles. See pages 116–117, for example.

- **POST-PREGNANCY CHALLENGE #7:**
  ## DISCOMFORT OR PAIN IN YOUR WRISTS •

Before pregnancy, you might have been accustomed to holding a heavy purse or lugging a gym bag. Suddenly, you are hoisting an extra ten, twenty, or even thirty pounds on an hourly basis as you carry your child and all the stuff that goes with him! Your back and shoulders are not the only body parts to bear the brunt of this added weight. Your wrists can become strained, too. You could be prone to carpal tunnel syndrome, a condition caused by excess pressure on a nerve in the wrist caused by edema, or swelling. Bending at your wrist can exacerbate this problem. You may experience numbness, tingling, or pain in your fingers, thumb, and hand when you push the stroller or hold baby. Carpal tunnel syndrome can appear during pregnancy or in the postnatal period.

WHAT YOU CAN DO ABOUT IT: Resting your wrists and maintaining proper wrist alignment when you pick things up or push your stroller can alleviate the problem. When you are pain-free, wrist flexion and wrist extension strengthening moves, along with stretches to the hand and fingers, can prevent further aggravation. Some breastfeeding moms notice that their pain recedes after weaning. *Lean Mommy* focuses on these and other subtle actions that can put pressure on a body that's already been taxed from pregnancy. See page 65.

- **POST-PREGNANCY CHALLENGE #8: NO TIME TO**
  ## EAT RIGHT OR TAKE CARE OF YOURSELF •

Eating can become a physical—and emotional—struggle for a new mom. From a practical perspective, you are so focused on taking care of baby and the rest of your family that your own mealtimes can be rushed or forgotten altogether. If you skip meals, you may be so famished that you head straight for the easiest thing to eat—fast food or a bag of cookies! At the same time, your awareness of your excess flab can trigger pangs of guilt: *Should I be eating this?* When it comes to fitting in workouts or time to relax, the same mental battles arise where you pit your welfare against that of your baby or family: *I need to exercise, but I can't leave baby.* Usually, you accept the sacrifice and tough it out. But putting self-care on hold completely can seriously impair a new mom's quality of life.

WHAT YOU CAN DO ABOUT IT: It's a fact that you now have less time than before. That's not going to change. But what you can change are your choices. You can choose foods that are nourishing *and* fast and easy to prepare. When you pack up baby wipes, you can throw in almonds and walnuts for yourself. When you mash up banana for your child, you can slice an extra piece for yourself and mix it with yogurt and oatmeal flakes. Or you can plan ahead what you're going to eat when eating out, so that you're less likely to succumb to the most fattening and least nutritious item on the menu.

And maybe you don't have time to work out. But you do have time to do what it takes to be a good mom. And when baby is crying his eyes out, you can entertain him or her by strapping him into his front-pack carrier and then doing a series of lower body toners like squats and lunges while you talk or sing him into a more joyful mood. (And voilà! there's your workout squeezed into your day.) Or you can give baby his dose of sunshine by joining other moms for a stroller walk around the park—an impromptu playgroup for the kids, and a much needed adult timeout for you. This way, mothering turns into me-time.

• POST-PREGNANCY CHALLENGE #9: TIRED ALL THE TIME •

Who knew you could get by on so little sleep? (Chances are, you're barely coping.) Although I was lucky to have help from my family after the birth of my children, I was reluctant to accept it because I felt such a strong need to bond with my babies. With all that waking up in middle of the night, I got so tired that I became totally disoriented, experiencing impaired vision, a feeling of being off balance, and extreme grumpiness! At times, the sheer exhaustion made me trip and knock into things and react sooooo slowly to everything. And while that only went on for months, it felt like years.

WHAT YOU CAN DO ABOUT IT: Short of hiring a full-time, live-in nanny and spending a full month under the covers catching up on

ZZZs, there's not much you can do to replenish lost sleep. Ideally, find a way to do shifts with your partner so you can at least get a solid block of shut-eye. But you can also enact some lifestyle changes that give you moments of rejuvenation. The *Lean Mommy* plan outlines quick Mommy Meditations to do when you need a mental recharge. I know you feel you don't have time to stop and meditate, but you'll be surprised at how much these few moments can help. Eating well and exercising can also help to rev you up when you need it.

• POST-PREGNANCY CHALLENGE #10: BABY BLUES •

What is known as the baby blues affects up to 80 percent of new moms within the first three weeks of having the baby, according to Postpartum Support International (PSI). You may feel weepy, moody, sad, anxious, and it may be difficult to concentrate. Up to 20 percent of new moms experience more severe depression, worry, and anxiety. A smaller percentage may progress to develop more serious mood disorders where they become obsessive, panicked, or even psychotic.

Any mood changes are a real problem and should not be ignored. Women don't often talk about this aspect of motherhood, because everyone expects you to be ecstatic about being a new mom. At the same time that you are supposed to be glowing with confidence over your new role, you may find yourself worrying that you are not up to the task, missing your old life, questioning whether you did the right thing, and feeling worthless because you are discovering that nursing isn't working as

"POSTPARTUM depression struck me out of the blue after my second child. I had always been healthy, positive, and active and I loved being a mom. But nothing could prepare me for the devastation of depression. It was more than just feeling sad. I was angry, miserable, irritable, and overwhelmed. When my baby was six months, I told my husband that I wanted a divorce and that he could have everything— the house, the kids, the car—as long as I could get some peace. He found a doctor who helped me with counseling and medication. As I recovered, I noticed that on the days that I exercised I was able to avoid a bad mood coming on. After my third baby, Lisa's program helped me avoid the recurrence of the postpartum depression."

—ADRIENNE GRIFFEN, 41,
mom of Claire, 7, John, 5, and Nora, 2,
Arlington, Virginia

well as it should. If you are really in a funk, you may even be reaching a low point where you neglect or hurt yourself or your child. This state can only exacerbate an already sinking body image, and you're likely to feel totally unmotivated to do much of anything, let alone get back into shape.

WHAT YOU CAN DO ABOUT IT: The hormone fluctuations and personal stresses that each mom experiences are unique. For serious depression, your doctor and a psychotherapist can provide the help you need. To help determine how serious your symptoms may be, you can use an online checklist (http://www.pndsa.co.za/ms-fc .htm). Most moms will experience at least some down moments, and I think that chronic sleep deprivation and utter exhaustion play a huge role. Trying to find ways to revitalize yourself can help. For minor cases of the baby blues, most doctors recommend exercise because of its mood-boosting effects.

Many new moms are told to avoid exposing their baby to germs. So they stay cooped up inside and avoid contact with people other than their immediate family. This will not only make you stir-crazy, but contribute to the onset of depression and sadness. Getting out of the house and socializing with other moms and babies can enhance the exercises' feel-good benefits.

What you eat can boost your energy. Many cells in your body do not work to their potential if you are lacking in nutrients. So making nutritious eating choices can help your body and your mind function in a more positive way. The *Lean Mommy* plan helps your well-being with positive eating and exercise experiences.

FACING POST-BABY REHAB HEAD-ON

Make sure to get your doctor's clearance before following the tips in the Lean Mommy *plan or before starting any other exercise program.*

You can begin by implementing the healthful eating strategies right away. You can instantly boost your body image by envisioning your wonderful mommy-body in a whole new healthy light! And when your doctor gives you the all-clear to start exercising, usually after six weeks, you can follow the *Lean Mommy* routines that address the changes that happened to your body while you were pregnant, such as saggy breasts, excess fat, and a flabby tummy. (Okay, there's not much I can do for your saggy breasts.) *Lean Mommy* also tackles your new functional needs; for example, since you will now spend much of your time hunched forward, whether it's from breastfeeding or hoisting a stroller, carrier, and car seat, you need to work on good spinal alignment. The goal of *Lean Mommy* is not just to show you what to eat and what kind of exercises to do, but for you to want to eat that way and to look forward to working out. And *Lean Mommy* will help you start to feel good about your body again (or for the first time!).

Get ready to enter a new phase of motherhood: Get ready to become a Lean Mommy.

"AFTER several miscarriages and a high-risk pregnancy, I became a first-time mom at forty and 260 pounds. Baby blues became postpartum depression. Medications and my therapist helped me realize that isolation was making me worse. My daughter and I attended Stroller Strides and our lives changed forever. Not only did the social support help, I lost seventeen pounds and worked up the courage to enter my first 10K walk/run. I still have seventy pounds to lose but I know that I will. And the best part is that other moms in class comment on how Caroline is always smiling and is the happiest baby they've seen. I chuckle to myself and think that I'm now the happiest mommy."

—ANGIE BERMAN, 41,
mom of Caroline, 2,
Glen Allen, Virginia

CHAPTER **2**

What You Think About the Way You Look

More powerful than any food you eat or any exercise you do, are your feelings about yourself. This chapter will help you break away from a negative body image so that you will be able to make—and stick to—positive lifestyle habits. This will not only make you happier, but you will be a better mom.

*A*fter having a baby, it's natural to want to lose the weight you gained. I've never met a mom yet (including myself) who likes the fleshy belly that's left after pregnancy. But it's important for your mental health not to be a slave to the scale. It's frustrating when your maternity clothes still fit better than your pre-pregnancy clothes. I remember looking at pre-pregnancy clothes after having my babies and thinking, "Did I ever really wear that?" Of course, when I did fit into those clothes, they didn't seem so little to me. It's all a matter of perspective.

How we see ourselves isn't always realistic. I once got on the scale and saw that I lost a solid five pounds. That made my week. At the end of that week, I got on the scale again. This time I was five pounds *heavier*. I was devastated. I hadn't noticed that I was gaining and had been feeling great about myself. I spent that whole day feeling fat and a little depressed. Then my husband mentioned that the scale had been knocked out of whack and that he had fixed it.

Whether I had gained, or even lost, suddenly became irrelevant. I was amazed (and embarrassed) that my own self-esteem could be so tied into the numbers on the scale. That my happiness with my day could be shaped by something so superficial sounds ludicrous— and it was. We all have feeling-fat days. But we need to try to banish them from our lives forever. We should measure ourselves by our energy, our health, and our inner beauty, not by numbers.

Of course, especially after having a baby, it's easy to slip into tunnel vision. If you have more fat on your bottom than you'd like, is that what you focus on? You don't *have* to. It's your choice whether you home in on what you don't like or whether you adopt a more accepting attitude and see the whole, healthy you. When you're depressed or unhappy, you are more likely to see only the negative. But you'll be happier if you focus on the positive.

During those post-pregnancy moments when all you see are thick thighs and a tubby tummy, remind yourself that your body is amazing—it grew a child! I remember one client who wore her stretch marks like badges of honor. Although the stretch marks may not be beautiful, her attitude was! If you have areas that you think need improvement, the first step in looking better is feeling better about the way you look *now.* And the way that you do that is to appreciate all the things that are great about you.

This is easier said than done. We're hypersensitive to our inadequacies, not just from the unrealistic body role models that bombard us through the media, but from images of celebrity moms who seem to gain little weight while pregnant (and are photographed looking glamorous the whole time). Then they seem to miraculously drop all baby weight immediately, sometimes within weeks of giving birth. Some of these women are genetically blessed. But some simply have a lifestyle that can support their recovery: chefs, personal trainers, nannies, and other help that enable them to get their body back fast. It gives us normal women an impossible standard to try to live up to.

It's easy to get sucked into this mind-set that we are somehow lacking if we aren't the perfect shape even if we've just had a baby and are busy with other things! It's easy to feel anxious and even desperate enough to want to go to extreme measures to get into pre-baby shape. You may diet yourself into delirium or fall for any fitness fad that promises to make you long and lean. Or you might succumb to liposuction or a breast augmentation. Or you may simply end up feeling guilty because as a busy mom, wife, and/or working woman, you are not doing enough to keep up.

But your self-esteem shapes your behavior. And if you feel bad about the way you look, you may try too hard with obsessive dieting and exercise. Or you may get de-motivated and not try at all and follow less-than-healthy eating and exercise habits. Either way, having a poor body image can trap you in a self-defeating cycle. It starts when you feel bad about yourself and decide to try to lose weight. You deprive yourself to do so. Deprivation leads to a desire for what you don't have. So you go out to dinner one night and succumb to forbidden foods. Or because you can't eat a slice of chocolate cake, you hold off until you can't resist and you later eat a whole one.

"I'VE been doing Stroller Strides for two years and am down to the weight that I was at sixteen! Plus I rarely have back pain anymore. And I now think about my body in terms of what it can do and what I can accomplish in it, rather than just how it appears to others."

—KIM KNOX, 33,
mom of Tyler, 3,
San Diego, California

And that's after you've eaten everything else in sight so you wouldn't eat the chocolate cake. Oops—the next day it's harder to regroup and get back on the diet. Or you get swamped at work and miss three workouts in a row. Oops—you were on a roll, but fall off and don't get back on again. Soon, it's two months since you last worked out and you're eating whatever is in front of you. And you feel disappointed, or even devastated, with yourself. If you lost weight at first, you gain it back. You may gain back even more. You feel worse and this increases your desire to lose weight. You may now be even more willing to try anything to do so. So you diet, you feel deprived, you overeat. This cycle goes on and on and is very hard to break.

What's worse is that this behavior is a normal way of life for many moms. Food becomes the enemy. Eating becomes a battle. For some, this self-defeating cycle may develop into a full-blown eating disorder (or it may resurrect a former one). For most everyone, it creates a life of disordered eating and exercise—you are constantly on the diet cycle, obsessing about your body and what you should (or shouldn't) eat.

As a mother, do you want to teach your children that going on and off diets is a normal way to live? Even if you feed your kids regular, normal meals, if they see you struggling and bouncing from cabbage soup to frozen diet dinners, or exercising to extremes, they will not only absorb your angst, they will learn your behavior.

Ironically, riding this roller coaster will not only fail to accomplish *permanent* weight loss or healthy body changes, it won't necessarily leave you looking better. Although I'm at a healthy weight now, I've cycled through many weights in my life. At my lowest weight, I was avoiding all fat. But my skin was full of ugly cysts. My hair was dry and brittle. And I was so run-down I'd catch every cold that came my way. At my skinniest, not only did I not feel very good, I didn't look very good and I wasn't happy. Beware of thinking that getting to a magic weight will bring you happiness.

If you are trapped in a cycle of self-hatred, before you start changing the way you eat or planning your exercise program, you need to reprogram your perceptions about your post-baby body. YOU are in charge of your body! YOU decide how you treat it. YOU decide whether you make it strong, or let it get weak, whether you eat for energy, or eat to deprive yourself.

You must stop thinking that you, or your body, or its parts are awful. At first, you may not be able to turn off the black thoughts, but you can lower the volume and try to scratch the record. You can redirect your self-talk by creating an awareness of it, then minimizing it—just don't let yourself dwell on your thighs. And when you catch yourself doing just that, change the negative message to a positive one.

When you learn to like and, hopefully, love your body, you will appreciate it. And that respect will trigger you to want to make the smart food and fitness choices that will help you reach your body goals. What's even better is that your children will learn to appreciate their bodies and their health because that's what they've learned from mom. The key is to get out of the mind-set that keeps you dwelling on what you don't like about yourself. It starts with the everyday habits that are holding you back.

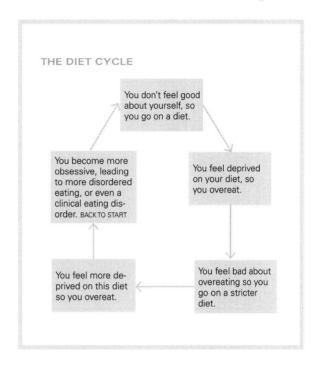

THE DIET CYCLE

You don't feel good about yourself, so you go on a diet.

You become more obsessive, leading to more disordered eating, or even a clinical eating disorder. BACK TO START

You feel deprived on your diet, so you overeat.

You feel more deprived on this diet so you overeat.

You feel bad about overeating so you go on a stricter diet.

FOCUS ON STRONG POINTS

Do any of the following sound familiar?

> You think tummy, you think FLAB.
> You think thighs, you think CELLULITE.
> You think butt, you think FAT.

Would you let your husband, your friends, or your children repeatedly call you fat, ugly, and flabby? Or would you call your friends, family, or children fat, ugly, or flabby? Then why would you do it to yourself? Every negative image boils down to telling yourself over and over that you are bad, bad, bad. Like a jingle that you can't get out of your head, a self-defeating thought takes root and becomes part of your everyday thought patterns. You deserve to treat yourself as well as you expect others to treat you and as you would treat others.

If you're going to pick apart your body, pick a part and think about how much it does for you. Each day, your eyes help you see your beautiful children, read a book, and get you through your day. *Appreciate* your stomach. Be grateful that you don't have reflux when you lie down, gas pains after meals, or cramping in the bathroom. If you appreciate feeling well, you'll be much more content with your body—and won't bash it as much.

BE WHAT YOUR LOVED ONES SEE

Your baby thinks you are the most beautiful creature to have ever walked the planet. (Your dog or cat does, too.) Allow yourself to see yourself through his or her eyes. Or see yourself as you would like your son or daughter to see him- or herself. Yes, he or she may have chubby thighs or baby acne, but don't you see beauty beyond that?

Create a rosy picture of yourself, too. When your child sees you, don't let him or her catch you with a worried or self-doubting expression because you feel flabby and self-conscious. Even if you don't yet believe that you are attractive, you need to start acting as if you do so that when your child sees you, he or she is presented with a smiling mom who looks strong, healthy, vibrant, and confident.

LOOK GENTLY IN MIRRORS

People who suffer from body discomfort either avoid looking in the mirror or they do so to focus critically on themselves. If you do shun mirrors, start looking in them. But before you do, identify something in your mind that you know you like about yourself. Focus on that when you glance at yourself. And monitor your response. If your first thought is, "Wow, where did that back fat come from?" try rephrasing it and noticing how the curve of your back is reminiscent of the beautiful women depicted in classic oil paintings. If you feel disgust at stretch marks across your belly, remember the beautiful baby that you grew in your amazing body and how it made room for that baby to grow. (Even if this exercise seems slightly ludicrous, try it.)

KEEP SCALES IN CHECK

Some women can weigh themselves and assess the feedback objectively. Many diet programs advocate weekly weighing to monitor weight gain and adjust eating and exercise behaviors accordingly. Weighing can be a good way to keep yourself on track.

But that's only if you can handle it. If you're prone to getting obsessive or having an emotional response to the numbers, throw your scale out the window. It can't measure your worth, your health, or your happiness. And do you want your children to mimic your behavior and start weighing themselves, too, as soon as they are able? If you feel the need to weigh yourself, do so infrequently and when you stumble on a number that you don't like, remind yourself that at the end of your life, your tombstone is not going to read, "Judy Smith, mother of three, weighing in at 135 pounds."

REFRAME SELF-DEFEATING THOUGHTS

You think diet, you think DEPRIVATION.
You think exercise, you think BORING or TORTURE.

Who can bother being active or eating well if it's penance for being so fat and flabby? If you do follow what feels like a punishing regimen, you're likely to fail since you're doing it for all the wrong reasons. If you hate your body, you will treat it badly. But if you respect and appreciate your body, you will *want* to treat it well because that is what makes you feel good.

It's not hard to train your mind to believe that you are sexy and attractive just as you are, or that good eating and exercise are enjoyable. It just takes *practice*. You can train your mind to believe anything, especially when it makes you feel good and has significant benefits like healthy eating and exercise.

WATCH WHAT YOU SAY

So many women engage in a feeding frenzy of negative reinforcement with their girlfriends and husbands, and they make comments in front of their kids. They talk about the body parts that bug them. They complain when they are feeling fat. They talk about diets and workouts and anything and everything that has to do with their bodies. Each and every remark ingrains body-bashing beliefs even deeper. But there are better ways to spend your time. In Stroller Strides classes, no one is allowed to make negative comments about their bodies or to talk about diets. Start listening to your conversations. And stop all the negative remarks. Practice thinking and speaking positive self-talk.

CHANGE YOUR TAPES

Our every behavior stems from the desire to feel good or to avoid feeling bad. If you think of healthy eating and working out as painful, and eating cookies and sitting on the couch as pleasurable, then you will choose to snack and sit. But if you can redefine your thoughts so that you think of being active as invigorating and eating well as energizing, as well as thinking that eating cookies is self-defeating, and not getting a daily dose of movement makes you sluggish, then you're likely to choose to engage in healthy lifestyle habits.

Imagine scenes from your life where you consistently react in a negative way that becomes self-defeating. Create a more positive response that will help you make the healthiest lifestyle choices. Practice changing your mental tapes every single day until those new thoughts become your new tapes. For example:

EXCUSE TO NOT EXERCISE	OVERCOME IT
I don't have time.	I have the same amount of time as other moms who fit in exercise. I'm going to schedule it so it fits in my life just like everything else.
I'm too tired.	Of course I'm tired. I didn't exercise. When I exercise, I have more energy to take care of baby and I sleep better.
I don't like to exercise.	If I don't feel like working out in a gym, I can take a walk with baby or find another activity that I enjoy. As I get better, I bet I will enjoy it more.

As you follow the *Lean Mommy* program, direct your energy toward boosting your body image and doing what it takes to follow a healthy lifestyle, rather than focusing on achieving a certain weight. Although you may want to lose all the weight as soon as possible, allow yourself about nine months. (Remember: It took you nine months to put the weight on.) Right now, your focus should be on your baby and your health. To make the smart choices that will change your behaviors and help you slim down, you must start by changing your attitudes, and you must stop tearing yourself down. If you can master the art of loving your body, the rest will come easy.

"I'VE learned how to have patience, and that is what leads to the commitment to keep working out. I've learned how to multitask and fit exercise into our busy schedules."

—LARA WOODWORTH, 30,
mom of Sabrina, 6, Olivia, 4,
and Nia, 5 months,
Surprise, Arizona

Increase your awareness of those behaviors that are sabotaging your self-esteem. If you can learn to be comfortable in your own skin and to appreciate your body for the good health you have, the energy it gives you, and your natural curves, you will become a Lean Mommy, and more importantly, you will be a happy mommy and a Lean Mommy who is a healthy role model for your child.

mommy meditation #1

Sit in a quiet upright position. Breathe quietly through your nose. Slow your breathing down and try to lengthen the time it takes you to exhale. Now imagine yourself in front of a mirror. See yourself as you are today. Scan the body and face that you know so well. Find an area that makes you uncomfortable. Stop and focus closer. Now soften the edges and see that body part blend in with the other curves in your face or on your body. Widen your perspective again so that you see the whole you, but soft and rounded and warm.

CHAPTER **3**

Know Thyself

Before getting into specifics, like what to eat or which exercise regimen to follow, you've got to get to the root of what drives you. This chapter will help you understand the triggers that lead you to make healthy or poor choices so that you can design a realistic program that you will stick to.

You know you should get out and work up a sweat. So why is it such a struggle? You know that eating the apple instead of the chips would be the better choice. So why are the chips so hard to resist?

There are several reasons: First, your habits are the result of a lifetime of experiences. And habits are hard to break. Many behaviors and thought processes started when we were young, often as a result of what our parents taught us, told us, or demonstrated. If you grew up with active parents, chances are you are active, too. But if you grew up with sedentary parents or parents who ate poorly, chances are you are, too.

Sometimes we resist making the right choices because it feels forced doing what doesn't jibe with our lifestyle. And so we rebel, even though we know we should be living healthier. Other times we're inspired to make the right choices, but we go down the wrong path. A mom's life is overloaded and we're often driven by bursts of energy. But since we're short on time and we want instant results, a quick fix lures us in. Our desire to change—and do it fast—can lead us to unrealistic expectations and poor choices. So we go for the two-week all-or-nothing diet, a month's worth of herbal fat-burning pills, or a seven-days-a-week intense workout schedule.

Making small changes is actually easier than dramatic over-hauls. But changing patterns and habits does take focus, patience, and practice. You won't get a quick fix this way. But you will get lasting results. Taking this approach isn't as simple as choosing a few specific foods to eat, or stumbling upon the right exercise. What you do is driven by your attitudes. So before you can change a behavior, you need to change how you think and feel about it. If you force yourself to do something that you don't really want to do, you may do it for a while, but you won't stick to it. If you change your mind-set to *want* to do it, you will and you will stick to it.

What will enable you to make this switch is known by psychologists as cognitive behavior therapy, or CBT. This approach includes cognitive therapy where you modify how you think about things. For example, if you grew up thinking that exercise was a chore and was hard, you probably still think of exercise in a negative light. If you shun workouts that you don't enjoy and find one that you do, you can overcome your unwillingness to do it. Behavior therapy modifies how you act. So instead of eating on the couch, you commit to only eating at the dining room table. These subtle changes end up making a big difference. Research has consistently shown that CBT results in higher weight losses and lower dropout rates than following a few rigid diet rules or an exercise routine alone.

Cognitive and behavior therapy includes monitoring your eating habits, identifying and controlling the stimuli that trigger you to crave food and eat it, modifying how and when you eat, rethinking self-defeating attitudes, learning more about exercise and good nutrition, and using mental training like meditation and visualization to help reinforce better patterns. It's about paying attention to the details of your daily behaviors and tweaking them to create better habits. This approach can feel boring since it involves making small changes rather than dramatic ones. Plus the process and the results are gradual. And because the process really is relatively painless, it can seem hard to believe that it's working. But it will if you commit to breaking old habits and creating new ones.

To determine which small lifestyle modifications will work for you, first you need to do a little homework to understand the thoughts, feelings, and motivations behind your eating and exercise patterns.

KEEPING A FOOD AND FITNESS DIARY

The most important tool in the behavior modification of your eating style and exercise habits is the Food and Fitness Diary. Before you can change your lifestyle behaviors, you need to become aware of them and this tool will help you do so.

The point here is not to make you crazy counting calories, but to provide a wake-up call so you realize what you are eating, when, and why. We tend to have a rosy recall of our behaviors: Research has shown that people think they eat healthier than they do or exercise more than they do. With the Food and Fitness Diary you'll have hard evidence. No more fuzzy recollections! Keeping track will help you notice that you skip meals often or that you went three days without a piece of fruit.

You must immediately record what you eat when you eat it (even—or especially—if it's a snack or a few pieces of candy from a colleague's desk). Be detailed and honest. Your most innocuous nibbles may be the most telling. For example, you may have had a "good" day eating and you recorded every morsel—everything that is, but the bag of M&M's you inhaled while in line at the store. That moment was important not to miss because this was when you ate as a reaction, not because that was what you planned to eat. Had you used your food diary, you might have noted that you went to the market hungry and let your blood sugar drop and the candy was a quick pick-me-up. Or you may have been angry that the line was so long, and that triggered you to eat to soothe your frustration. So keep track of every meal and snack.

You only need to record what you eat for one week. I know you think you know yourself, but you'll be surprised at how much more you learn about your eating patterns by writing them on paper. Most people stay on track very well during the week, but feel like they lose control over the weekend. You can prevent weekend binges if you can identify what triggers them, and this tool will help. In a traditional behavior modification program, you keep a food diary for an extended period. We will assume that as a time-crunched mom, this will only further stress your life. So, just do it for one week so you can identify your eating style.

If you're a brand-new mommy and still in survival mode taking care of your little one, postpone this exercise. Your primary goal now is to fuel your body and take care of yourself and your little one(s). When you feel you are ready to better understand your eating style, then give it a try.

The food diary doesn't just track what you are eating but who you are eating with because your environment often affects your choices. Consider your weekly Thursday night dinner with your friend Mary where you inevitably end up stuffing in four margaritas and two bowls of chips. If you chose a different place to eat, would you eat more sensibly? Or is Mary the problem—does being with her somehow encourage you to binge? Is she an old college friend that puts you in a let-loose mood? Maybe you should meet Mary for a power walk, or you could invite her over to dinner. Or perhaps you shouldn't go out with Mary for a little while until you get control over your ability to resist temptations.

By first identifying your behaviors, you can analyze them and change them to produce a better result for yourself. Some people find that keeping a food diary on a pretty regular basis helps keep them on track. If this is the case for you, then do so. But I don't want you to get overly focused on every morsel that enters your lips. This diary is to make you cognizant, not cuckoo. To get started on your *Lean Mommy* plan, photocopy the form on page 29 or get out a clean notebook and start your own diary to track what your patterns have been up to now.

HOW TO USE THE FOOD AND FITNESS DIARY

1. Write when you eat and where you eat.
2. Note your feelings before the meal (you will also record your feelings afterward).
3. Rate your hunger level according to the scale below at the start and end of each meal or snack. Sometimes we eat when we are not hungry, overeat when we are full, or let ourselves get too hungry before we do eat. This may be tied to different feelings or environments surrounding the meal. A key to healthful eating is knowing when to eat and when to stop eating.

HUNGER SCALE

1	2	3	4	5
Starving	Hungry	Satisfied/ Not Hungry	Full	Stuffed

4. Under "Meal/Activity" note if you are eating a meal or a snack. Also include exercise. Record real workouts such as going for a run or doing a fitness DVD. And make note of nonexercise active periods where you are moving fifteen minutes or longer, such as taking the baby and dog out for a walk or strolling around the mall.
5. Be very specific with food descriptions and portion sizes. The more specific you can be, the better: You may

FOOD AND FITNESS DIARY (sample morning)

DAY	TIME	PLACE	FEELINGS BEFORE	HUNGER SCALE	MEAL/ ACTIVITY	FOOD AND PORTIONS	OTHER PEOPLE	FEELINGS AFTER	HUNGER SCALE
Monday	8 a.m.	Car	Rushed	1	Breakfast	1 banana, 1 black coffee	Kids in the car	Rushed, a little hungry	
	10 a.m.	Kitchen	Sleepy, busy	3	Snack	10 animal cookies, 18 oz. glass of water	Katie (2-year-old)	Disappointed I ate the cookies and so many of them	
	12 noon	Couch	Tired	4	Lunch	Sandwich: 2 slices turkey, 2 slices cheddar cheese, 1 tbsp mayo, sourdough bread; 1 can Diet Coke; 5 small pretzels	Alone, baby is asleep	Tired	
	1 p.m.	Outside	Tired	3	Activity	Walked with baby around the block for 30 minutes	Ann, neighbor mom	Hot but invigorated; nice to get out and talk; glad I did it	

FOOD AND FITNESS DIARY

DAY	TIME	PLACE	FEELINGS BEFORE	HUNGER SCALE	MEAL/ ACTIVITY	FOOD AND PORTIONS	OTHER PEOPLE	FEELINGS AFTER	HUNGER SCALE

want to enter the information later into a food database such as the one at the USDA's MyPyramid.gov to get a nutritional breakdown of your days. Include brand names of foods, or ingredients for restaurant dishes.

6. List who was with you when you ate, and if it was for a special occasion.

7. Record your feelings after your snack or meal.

Keep track of everything you eat for *at least* five days, including weekends. If you can do it for seven days, or up to fourteen, you will get a more accurate picture of your eating patterns. Avoid changing your eating habits; try not to eat better than normal for now. Be aware that it's natural to start to do this because as you begin to keep track you will become more aware of poor choices. But save the eating changes for later. Right now you want to use this as a tool to identify your typical behaviors.

Now make photocopies of the blank Food and Fitness Diary on page 29 or mark out the appropriate columns in a notebook. Make sure to carry this around with you at all times.

After one week of using the diary, start looking for patterns that seem to trigger overeating or skipping exercise. Brainstorm ways to improve upon them using the questions below. Right now you're just brainstorming. You'll get more specific suggestions in the following chapters.

ANALYSIS	MY PATTERN	SOLUTION
Do you tend to eat more when people are with you?		
Are you skipping meals?		

ANALYSIS	MY PATTERN	SOLUTION
Chart the number of times you eat at different points in the hunger scale. Try always to stay between 2 and 4 on the scale.		
How many hours is the longest gap between eating?		
Do you do this more than once per day?		
Chart the times when you feel upset, depressed, or rushed, with the food you ate at that time. Is there a pattern?		
How many servings of fruit do you eat on average every day?		
How many servings of vegetables do you eat on average every day?		
How often do you fit in regular workouts?		

(*continued on next page*)

ANALYSIS	MY PATTERN	SOLUTION
How active are you (not including workouts) every day?		
Is there anything that jumps out at you that you can improve upon?		
Are you drinking at least 64 ounces of water per day?		
Ask yourself: What days did I feel best about my eating? How can replicate that?		
Other:		
Other:		

ARE YOU A STRESS EATER?

Notice that a key element of the food diary is linking what you eat with what you're feeling at the time you eat it. Very often we use overeating or eating certain foods to cope when we feel challenged or out of control. Or we might make poor meal choices because we are simply too frantic to stop and consider what we really want or should eat.

Stress is a part of life that's not going away. Sometimes, it's even a component to our success. And both positive and negative types of stress can still make you anxious. There is no one perfect way to respond when you start feeling tension in your life. If you use food as a panacea, find other ways to deal with your problems. A better coping mechanism to diffuse stress is exercise.

WHERE YOU WENT WRONG IN THE PAST

Recall your history of weight loss attempts. Remember as much as you can about what prompted you to follow a certain diet or exercise program:

1. Note the time of year or period in your life that you followed each plan. New Year's? Just before the summer or a wedding?
2. Why did you start the plan? What was your goal? What were you unhappy with?
3. What did you do? Describe the rules you had to follow.
4. How long did you stick to it?
5. What were your feelings about the experience and the outcome?
6. How much weight or how many inches did you lose, and how long did it take?
7. How much weight or how many inches did you gain back, and how long did it take?
8. Can you now see stumbling blocks that led to your failure that you could not see then?
9. If you were to improve upon what you did each attempt, what would you do differently now that might ensure your success?

DIET HISTORY

DATE	WHY	WEIGHT LOSS ATTEMPT	RULES	HOW LONG?	FEELINGS	WEIGHT LOSS	WEIGHT GAIN	MISTAKES	SOLUTIONS

SETTING GOALS FOR SUCCESS

Goal-setting can be tricky because a goal can set you up for success—or failure. Most people easily come up with grand plans. For instance, they say they want to lose all their pregnancy weight in three months, or they plan to work out five days a week the moment their doctor gives the six-week clearance. These goals may be reachable—eventually. But they are so lofty that they can be unrealistic. If a new behavior doesn't fit into your lifestyle, is too much to keep up with, or doesn't provide you with motivating feedback along the way, you simply won't achieve your goal. You may make a valiant effort, but the odds are against your success. And failure not only doesn't get you what you want, it can de-motivate you. (Aren't you already a little tired at the thought of trying to go on another diet?) But if you choose a realistic goal, divvy it up into doable chunks, and give it time, you're likely to succeed.

If you are reading this book, you are probably still battling the weight put on during pregnancy. If you are driven to lose weight, what does that mean to you? Do you want to see a specific number on your scale? Do you want to get into a certain pair of jeans? Or do you just want to look better? Do you feel that you will be more desirable or liked if you are thinner? Some people want to lose weight to have enough energy to play with their children. Others want to be able to get out and do things, enjoy people, and live.

My hope is that you change your goals so that they are not weight loss or vanity related but are instead empowering—health and energy motivated or related to how you want to inspire your children. Empowering goals can lead you to the results you want (to look better and lose weight), but with a higher chance of success. When trying to define exactly how you want to improve your body shape, keep in mind that your ideal weight is:

- One that you can keep for a lifetime (within five pounds).
- One that has sufficient toned muscle mass and a body-fat percentage in a healthy range.

- One that allows you to participate in all of life's activities.
- One that makes you feel healthy, comfortable, and alive.

A common method of creating goals is to use the SMART approach. SMART is an acronym for the characteristics of effective goals. I have modified it just a bit to fit my philosophy. Your goals should be Specific, Measurable, Achievable, Reinforceable, and Timely.

Specific—Clearly define what you want to happen.

Measurable—How can you know if you did it if you can't tell a difference? Your goal needs to be something that can be measured.

Achievable—Aim for something that is possible. Yes, it can be a reach, but it needs to be within the realm of your personal possibility.

Reinforceable—Is it something that you can reinforce and reward yourself for?

Timely—Is there a time frame to accomplish the goal?

Ideally, you want a grand goal that encompasses all these components, and subgoals that fit this model, too. No goal is too small as long as it helps you to progress. Here are examples using (and not using) the SMART approach:

	NOT-SO-SMART GOAL	SMART GOAL
Example 1	I want to eat healthier.	I want to eat 15 grams of fiber each day. (Subgoal: I will eat beans for lunch every day and a piece of fruit with every meal.)

	NOT-SO-SMART GOAL	SMART GOAL
Example 2	We will eat at home more.	We will only eat out two times per week. (Subgoal: I will pre-make four healthy meals on Sundays for my family so that they are ready-made for the week.)
Example 3	I am going to start running.	I will run three times per week and will be ready to run a half-marathon in six months. (Subgoal: I'm going to run three times per week and train for a 5K in three months.)

To make your goals more effective, identify the passion that motivates them so that they hold the power to move you. Achieving your goal has to give you great pleasure, and not achieving your goal has to give you great pain. If your goal doesn't evoke this sort of strong emotional response, it simply won't work. Your vision of your desired lifestyle will keep you motivated. So elucidate your vision as clearly as possible.

HOW LONG SHOULD GETTING BACK IN SHAPE TAKE? HOW HARD SHOULD YOU WORK?

The first few months after baby is born are not a time to focus on weight loss. Your body has gone through so much and now you're consumed with the awesome labor of taking care of a new baby. You don't need to diet and over-exercise. You do need to eat for energy

GOALS LACKING PASSION	GOALS WITH PASSION
I want to lose weight.	I want to lose weight so that I can be healthy for my next pregnancy.
I want to stop eating fast food.	I want to make healthy eating choices so that I set a good example for my children.
I want to exercise five days per week.	I want to exercise five days per week because it keeps my back pain at bay.

and exercise for stamina. If you do, I promise that you will lose that weight and you will feel good.

Even if you think that you need to lose fifty pounds, it's better to shoot for a lower goal, say, ten pounds. If you just had a baby, I understand that ten pounds does not even sound close to okay. But it's harder to stick to a bigger goal. If you shoot for ten, you can reap the reward faster and progress to a follow-up goal of losing another ten pounds.

If you have always been super-fit and in good shape, you may feel a strong urge to push to get back to the way you were. Our culture is so competitive and driven that sometimes we see stepping back as defeat. But what you've been through is one of the biggest physiological processes your body may ever experience. Take a deep breath and relax and give yourself time. When you were pregnant, chances are that you gave yourself permission and understanding about your body widening in girth. Extend that permission and that acceptance for just a bit longer so you can recover and restrengthen and rebuild.

Now, keeping all these insights about yourself in mind, read the rest of the book to find out ways to reach fitness and food goals. Then return to this section and follow the steps below. Set a motivating and realistic larger goal comprised of concrete and achievable sub-goals. Post your goal and the plans to achieve it in your organizer and on your refrigerator—anywhere that you will see it every day so it is not forgotten. Use the following questions to create your goal. As you read through the book and across new ideas to better shape your goal and how you will achieve it, revisit these questions and more clearly define your strategy.

1. Choose a goal.
2. Figure out what you need to do to achieve this.
3. How long will it take realistically?
4. Is what you need to do practical?
5. Can the steps needed fit into your lifestyle? What will you adjust about what you do now exactly?
6. Establish some mini-goals.
7. Set a time frame and action plan for each.
8. Determine how you will assess when and if you've reached each mini-goal.

You can accomplish ANYTHING if you break it down into a gradual, achievable plan! If you committed every single day to taking a baby step to progress toward a goal, those baby steps would add up. In a year you might not even recognize your life.

What if you lapse or slip back into old habits? Do you throw in the towel? Beat yourself up? No. Just get up, refocus on your goal, and start again. Consider it to be a part of maintaining balance and moderation: No one is perfect all the time. As a mom, you've seen or will see your children learn to walk. It can take months for your little one to get from first steps to walking with confidence. They fall ten times a minute when learning. Would you ever encourage your child to give up, be critical, or decide, "Oh I guess my baby can't learn to walk"? Of course not! You know that if they keep trying, they will

CHAPTER 4

Nuts and Bolts Fitness

You shouldn't even think about losing the baby weight without thinking about fitness. You don't have to do killer workouts. But you do have to move every day to strengthen areas weakened by pregnancy and to develop stamina for motherhood. This chapter spells out the basics about fitness.

Many women worry that it's not possible to regain their pre-pregnancy figure or that they'll forever have that pregnant pooch. The funny thing about getting in shape after you have a baby is that some women surpass their wildest expectations. I know many women who have had one or more babies and are in the best shape of their lives. It took time, but they did it. I've seen it over and over again: Even if you've never been in shape, now, for the first time in your life, you can be! The most successful moms in Stroller Strides have not been those who were super-athletic, or the ones who lived at the gym and were in perfect shape before. Some were even overweight and out-of-shape before they got pregnant.

What did the trick is that these women started walking and

targeting the areas that were compromised in pregnancy. And as part of the Stroller Strides program they discovered a social element to an activity that was easy to do. Many of these women realized for the first time ever that they actually liked to exercise and that it could easily fit into their lifestyle. So they kept coming. They stuck to it. That's the secret: Moms who see results from exercise are those who do it and keep doing it.

The women who see the most dramatic changes from exercise are those who are active five or six times a week. This may seem impossible. But not every workout has to be a bona fide workout. If you play with your kids vigorously you'll work up a sweat and burn extra calories. You can also turn cleaning up and everyday errands into a workout.

In today's sedentary culture we sit at desks, on sofas, or in cars for most of the day. All the calories we're not burning have nowhere to go except to be stored as fat. At the same time, not using our bodies much makes our muscles weak, too. Hence, not only can you have cellulite (accumulated fat), but flab, too.

Quick! Let's do a healthy-body-image check. Bodies can get out of shape from disuse. But in no way am I encouraging you to dislike your body, your body parts, or yourself because of it. So even though we will focus on areas that need help, resist the urge to judge yourself negatively. Be informed about the important areas to work on, but don't focus on what's weak, focus on strength.

Body changes can happen so gradually that they go unappreciated. So take a moment now to take stock of your starting point. As you get fitter, notice

"I became obese, depressed, and slept all the time after graduating from college. After having a baby, I could not bring myself to exercise. Then someone invited me to Stroller Strides. It saved my life. Before, I could barely get out of bed, now I can keep up with the other mothers and even jog a little. I have so much more energy and I'm excited to be alive!"

—JENNY LUTKINS, 31,
mom of Wyatt, 1,
Franklin, Tennessee

"EXERCISING with other moms kept me motivated and helped me stick to it."

—JESSICA CRUZ, 22,
mom of Quintin, 2,
Kingsland, Georgia

the narrowing of your waist, the hint of definition at your arm, and the new tone of your thighs. Consider taking pictures and measurements, not to focus on weight loss, but to realize later that you have truly improved your body. The best proof is how you feel on the inside, but sometimes external reinforcement can help.

"I went from career woman to stay-at-home mom practically overnight. I experienced some postpartum depression, but Stroller Strides helped me get on a positive track. I was never much into exercise before, but now I'm in better shape than I have been in the past ten years—and that's after three kids! The hardest part is fitting it in. But since this is a play date as well as a workout, I'm doing it for my children as well as myself."

—APRIL SOLIS, **39,**
mom of Miguel, 3, and Julian, 2,
San Diego, California

WHAT YOU NEED TO DO FOR SUCCESS

To enhance weight loss and keep it off, you must be active. So what type of exercise should you do and how much? I'll explain the official recommendations, then we'll do a reality check because you may have to modify these prescriptions based on the practical aspects of being a mom. To be physically fit, a person should be strong in several areas.

CARDIO

WHAT IT MEANS

Having a strong cardiovascular system means that your heart and lungs work efficiently and that you are able to deliver oxygen throughout your body effectively. You become better at burning body fat and can lower blood pressure, improve cholesterol, increase insulin sensitivity, and even experience a boost in your sex drive! The kind of exercise that provides the stimulus for cardiovascular improvements is aerobic exercise, also known as cardio.

WHICH EXERCISES?

Cardio activity is moving your whole body at once and over a period of time using the major muscle groups that will get your heart rate up and raise your body temperature. You huff and puff a little and you work up a sweat.

Walking, running, jumping, cycling, skating, swimming, cardio machines like the elliptical trainer, dancing, aerobics, and similar activities are all true cardio activities. Sports that incorporate walking, running, and jumping also are considered cardio. These include tennis, volleyball, soccer, basketball, racquetball, squash, softball, playing tag, kickball, and so on. Picking up toys, vacuuming, or washing floors and windows can be turned into a cardio activity if you put enough energy behind them.

You may have heard—and been confused over—the terms "aerobic" and "anaerobic." These are physiological terms that describe how the fuel is being metabolized in your body when you are moving. When you're working aerobically, you can sustain an activity like walking for an extended period of time. When you work anaerobically, you can only sustain the activity for a short duration such as when sprinting, weight-lifting, or jumping. Within any one workout you can work both aerobically and anaerobically depending upon how hard you push. It's a good idea to train both systems by altering the intensities of your workouts.

BURNING FAT VS. BURNING CARBS

Your body burns mostly a mix of fat and carbohydrates for energy. So whenever you are burning calories you are burning both of these fuels. (Some people believe that you use protein for energy. Protein is not a primary fuel source unless you are in a starvation state, for example.) It is rare to burn only fat or only carbohydrates. To burn fat, carbohydrates in the form of glucose need to be used in the biochemical process.

But carbs provide a quicker energy source. So when you need to produce force or power, carbs are better able to provide the energy to do it. Fats are more efficient (and even the skinniest of us have a more abundant supply of fat compared to carbs in our bodies). So when you are in a stable energy state, fat becomes the predominant energy source.

To put this in practical terms: Generally when you're sitting, you don't require much quick energy, so you burn mostly fat (but still some carbs). But you are only burning about one calorie per minute (you are sitting, after all). When you start walking at a stroll-like pace, you aren't pushing too hard, so your body still uses predominantly more fat (but is still using carbs). You are now burning maybe four or five calories per minute. If you pick up the pace and walk briskly, you may still be burning mostly fat, but the ratio may shift a little to help you process fuel faster. And you might now be burning about six calories per minute. If you were to break into a sprint, suddenly you can't burn fat fast enough, so quick-acting carbs need to kick in. The ratio of fuel shifts again to provide the energy you need. So now you may be burning predominantly carbs, but still some fat. If you jump, the same thing occurs. You now may be burning eight or nine calories per minute.

There is often confusion because many people believe that you burn less fat when you work anaerobically. That misconception is the result of misunderstanding the physiology. The bottom line is, for weight loss it doesn't matter which kind of fuel you burn. The body always shifts between burning different ratios of fat and carbohydrates. But this is not that important because what's important is the total calories you burn. You burn fat during all cardio workouts, no matter what. And you burn more total calories when you move faster or work harder. The more you burn, the more fat you lose. Burning BOTH fat calories and carb calories can result in fat loss or pounds off the scale. So working at higher levels of aerobic intensity, or incorporating anaerobic sprints into a low- or moderate-intensity workout, gives you an extra calorie-burning boost.

Of course, not everyone is fit enough to push super-hard. So you can accumulate a sizable calorie burn in two ways. You can either work harder in a shorter amount of time. Or you can work longer at an easier pace. Beginners tend to prefer taking an easier approach. Experienced exercisers are better equipped at challenging themselves and working harder. I suggest taking the easier approach simply because you're more likely to stick with it!

HOW MUCH?

Much research has been conducted investigating how much exercise a person needs to do. It really depends on your goal. Even small amounts of exercise are great for your *health*. Just moving a little every day, even for fifteen or thirty minutes, can improve metabolic functions like how sensitive your body is to insulin and how it reacts to excess blood sugar as well as reduce your risks of heart disease and other chronic conditions. That's why the U.S. Centers for Disease Control and Prevention and the American College of Sports Medicine recommend that all healthy adults accumulate thirty minutes of moderate-intensity activity on most, if not all, days of the week. Although all types of exercise count, generally the recommendations reflect more cardio activity than lower-calorie-burning activities like strength work or stretching. So that means on, say five days of the week, you'll meet the quota if you walk with your baby in the stroller at a brisk pace for thirty minutes. Or you can even take two shorter walks a day for fifteen minutes each.

WEIGHT LOSS WITH SHORT WORKOUTS VS. LONGER WORKOUTS

Some women can drop baby weight from this amount of exercise, although some need more. If you work a little harder in that thirty minutes, say you run rather than walk or push baby up hills to increase intensity, you will burn more calories and that will have an even bigger effect. If you have not been active before, then doing thirty minutes of low-intensity activity would still probably help you lose weight.

The less cardio activity you do, however, the slower the weight loss is. And that's because it's mostly a numbers game. In thirty minutes of moving around, you might burn 150 to 300 calories. (How many depends on how hard you work and how heavy you are. The heavier you are, the more calories you burn because your body needs more energy to move the extra weight. As baby gets bigger and the stroller gets heavier, that will increase your workload and the amount of calories burned.)

But, theoretically, it takes burning around 3,500 calories to lose one pound of fat. So, you're going to have to do enough workouts at say 150 calories burned per session, to add up to 3,500 calories, or 7,000 calories for two pounds of fat, and so on. Obviously this would be nearly impossible to do in a short amount of time. Here is one more reason why living the lean lifestyle long-term works. If you do that thirty-minute walk every single day for two weeks, then you might burn 2,100 calories, not even a pound of fat. But if you did that same short walk every day for a year, you'd burn nearly 55,000 calories and you could lose up to fifteen pounds! Combining easy calorie reduction from what you eat, like cutting out 100 calories every day in small ways, with regular activity will add up, and in the long term, produce dramatic results!

Most people can't wait one year. Also, different people have different physiological makeups. So this theoretical caloric equation may not work perfectly in every body. For example, people who were overweight (not from pregnancy), and then lose the extra weight, tend to have a tougher time losing more weight or keeping it off because of many factors that make their body want to regain lost fat, and hold on to it tighter.

That's why more recent research has established more realistic fitness guidelines for losing weight or maintaining weight loss. The Institute of Medicine and the USDA's Dietary Guidelines recommend that a person do sixty to ninety minutes of accumulated moderate-intensity physical activity at least five days per week. Yes, this may

"BEFORE getting pregnant, I smoked and was overweight. Having a baby motivated me to get active. Now I have a six-pack! And I'm such a good example: My three-year-old imitates doing squats and lunges. I grew up thinking that exercise was something you had to do to keep from being fat—but my kids see it as something fun to do with your friends and family."

—SUMMER HIXON, 28,
mom of Aubrianna, 3,
San Diego, California

"BECAUSE I was over thirty-five and had nearly died in a car accident with a drunk driver, I was considered an at risk pregnancy and advised not to exercise. I joined Stroller Strides after my first child, and now three years later, I am the fittest that I have ever been in my life. My kids wake up and beg to go. You see, not only do I fit a workout in, all the moms and kids sing, play, and blow bubbles."

—DANA PUSTINGER, 40

mom of Sara Ann, 4, and Jack, 2, San Marcos, California

sound undoable. But, you can figure out ways to fit it in in chunks—partly through bona fide workouts, and partly through everyday mommy activities like playing with your kids.

To understand how much bigger an impact these guidelines make, look at the numbers again. Let's say you walk for a total of 1 hour and 15 minutes every day. That means, instead of burning, say, 150 calories for a 30-minute walk, you'd burn around 375 (remember, calories vary). Walking every day for two weeks would burn about 5,250 calories, and you'd theoretically lose about 1 pound and one half (and more if you incorporate small diet improvements to cut calories a little more). Along with this loss you would start to see some fat loss on your body, too. So you can see how doing a little bit more produces faster results. But the real rewards come over time. If you did this longer walk on just five—instead of seven—days a week for a full year, then you'd burn over 97,000 calories and could theoretically lose 28 pounds! And adding smart eating improvements can bump up that number even more.

Notice in the chart on the right how even everyday activities can burn extra calories to help you to lose weight!

MUSCLE

WHAT IT MEANS

There is a difference between just moving your body—which requires moving your muscles—and working targeted muscles specifically. Although cardio exercise is great overall and is the best way to burn calories, it does not strengthen specific muscles. (If you work

EXERCISE CALORIE BURN

PHYSICAL ACTIVITY	CALORIES BURNED IN 30 MINUTES
Stroll the neighborhood	162
Brisk walk on the school track	249
Swing, slide, and climb with kids at playground	198
Play soccer in the park	495
Ride a bike	396
Hike in the fields or woods	297
Swim in a cool pool	495
Play tag, hide-and-seek, duck-duck-goose	249
Jump rope in the grass	495
Skate on the sidewalk	208
Shoot hoops in the driveway	222
Toss a football in the backyard	123
Walk to the grocery store	162
Toss a Frisbee	150
Grab a court, hit tennis balls	348
Find the hose, wash the car	150
Mow the lawn	297

hard like hiking up hills or cycling against heavy wind, you will gain some strength in your lower body, but overall, cardio exercise is not meant to produce muscle-strengthening, but more muscle stamina.)

If you work particular muscles against resistance and challenge them to work harder than normal, they will respond over time by becoming stronger. When they become stronger, they also become firmer. So, what keeps you strong enough to lift baby are strong muscles. And what keeps flab at bay are strong muscles.

When muscles are stretched, you can increase your flexibility in a tight muscle as well as the surrounding joint. (Not many people realize that you also increase your flexibility by doing resistance exercises.) Flexibility is important, although because it doesn't burn many calories, it doesn't have a major effect on helping you lose weight. However, we lose flexibility as we age, and stretching helps you retain it, so it's important to include in your weekly routine. (Plus, it sure feels good!)

WHICH EXERCISES?

There are many approaches to strengthen specific muscles. Usually you do a move that makes the muscle contract and you feel a burn. But some moves can be misleading because a burn doesn't always signify that you are targeting the muscle in a way that makes it stronger. The most effective way to strengthen muscles is by lifting weights or using rubber tubing or elastic bands for resistance. You can also use your own body weight in some instances.

Strengthening moves generally burn fewer calories than cardio activity. But if you focus on the larger lower body muscles and keep the moves continuous, you may be able to bump that up a bit. However, the calorie burn is not necessarily the point of this type of exercise—the aim is to develop strength and muscular endurance.

The *Lean Mommy* plan uses rubber tubing, which you can get at any sporting goods store or from fitness product companies online (including my Web site, www.strollerstrides.com). Since tubing is so light and portable, you can store it in your stroller or car and whip it out at any time. I've also devised a series of exercises using your baby as your weight. By strapping him or her into the front-pack carrier, you create a weighted vest. Suddenly, moves like squats and lunges become much more challenging!

Yoga, Pilates, and similar movement regimens use body weight for strength and balance. This can be challenging, and depending on the move, a good way to develop stability and certain kinds of strength. Many of the moves may also incorporate some stretching and meditation.

HOW MUCH?

The American College of Sports Medicine guidelines recommend resistance training one to three days per week, with a day of rest in between. You can strength train more frequently if you work different muscles each day. Flexibility exercises should be done two to three days per week.

The benefits of exercise go beyond body fat and weight control. As well as improving your overall health, you'll also find that you have more energy during the day. Being a Lean Mommy can be exhausting—but if you train for the job by keeping fit, you'll find that you have the stamina to keep up with your sweetie! In the next chapter, you'll learn about those areas that moms need to strengthen and practical ways to integrate more activity into your busy life.

CHAPTER **5**

Moms on the Move

Most new moms find that exercise drops to the bottom of their priority list. But it's essential to fit it in and adapt your workouts to the changes and challenges of motherhood. This chapter addresses your mom-specific fitness needs so you can become better, buffer, and stronger than ever before.

People don't realize how much physical work is involved in being a mom. You're lugging a (cute) little weight around all day. And you're also lugging all of his or her (not-so-cute) accessories. There's constant picking up, bending down, and twisting all around. As if being pregnant and giving birth to the baby doesn't batter your body enough, these new physical exertions can really take a toll. More changes happen to your body in nine months of pregnancy than will happen to a man's body in his entire life. And to top it off, afterward when you are weak and de-conditioned, you are expected to carry around a ten- to twenty-pound baby all day long.

As outlined in Chapter 1, there are many physical after-effects of pregnancy. Your posture may have withered, your back may ache, and in addition to excess flab, you may have separated abdominal muscles. You may be experiencing uncontrolled urination or constant urges to urinate. I've designed the *Lean Mommy* plan to account for all of your post-pregnancy needs. Each workout that follows includes the necessary exercises to strengthen what's weak, stretch what's tight, tone up what's flabby, and lean down what's mushy.

WHEN TO START?

The American College of Obstetricians and Gynecologists recommends resuming exercise as soon as it is physically and medically safe. Generally, your doctor will give the all-clear to start exercising about six weeks after birth. If you had a C-section or a severe episiotomy, you may need to wait a little longer.

WHAT TO DO: WEEKS 0 TO 6

In the first few days, you can begin doing pelvic floor exercises, known as Kegels (see pages 63–65). You may resume gentle activity such as walking and stretching, and start light abdominal reconditioning such as abdominal bracing (see pages 58–60). You can go on short walks (five to fifteen minutes) after about two to four weeks.

Overall, keep it gentle for the first six weeks. Your goals during this time are to rest and recover from childbirth, and to bond with your baby. If you are nursing, you'll find that an ungodly amount of hours will be spent with your baby literally attached to you. My husband would jokingly make moo sounds whenever he passed the nursery.

Key activities to avoid are those that may stress your wounds from a C-section or episiotomy, or that may exacerbate overly flexible joints. Avoid wide lunges and squats, or big lateral movements such as wide pliés. Hold off on jumping, jogging, ab crunches, or any moves that may increase intra-abdominal pressure on your pelvic floor or back. Stop immediately if any exercise causes pain, increased bleeding, dizziness, or fatigue.

Lochia, your vaginal discharge after pregnancy, normally lasts about six weeks. A sure sign that you're overexerting yourself or exercising too much is lochia that is bright red or pink or increases after it had started to taper off.

Fatigue can be a major issue for you now. You'll be in survival mode for the first six months, for sure. If you're lucky, your baby may start sleeping six or seven hours by the three-month mark. Unfortunately, those probably aren't the same hours during which you are resting. Beyond sleep deprivation, your body is recuperating from pregnancy, childbirth, and your new life as a mom. So, take it easy. Find light activities that will give you energy, not become an additional burden to your body. If after doing an activity you feel even more exhausted, then you know you pushed it too hard.

WHAT TO DO: WEEK 6 AND BEYOND

Once your doctor clears you to exercise, you can embark on any of the *Lean Mommy* workouts in this book. I've divided them into two levels, depending upon whether you are exercising for the first time, or worked out regularly before pregnancy. Both levels start you slow and build you up gradually. And remember, your workouts are not meant to be a quick fix. It took you nine months to gain the weight, and it may take as long to take it off. In addition to aiding weight loss, your workouts will strengthen you psychologically and physiologically.

THE EXERCISE TRAP

As is the case with dieting, you can have too much of a good thing when it comes to exercise. Some women take exercise to extremes when they start a new program. This can backfire in several ways.

If you do too much too soon, or work out too hard before your body is ready for it, you are likely to get burned out or injured. Exercise shouldn't hurt to be effective. Remember, this is a lifestyle change: You need to start with the small additions to your day, and work your way up. Your workouts should always be easy enough that you develop a sense that you *can* do them. If it's a struggle, you will find it hard to persevere. You need to start slow and increase gradually as your body gets stronger. Sometimes, this isn't so easy for moms who were extremely fit before they got pregnant. They want to push harder than they are ready to. Take baby steps.

Over-committing at first is also a big no-no. You may be able to obsess over a new workout for a week or two. But if it interferes with your family time, chances are that you'll quit sooner rather than later. That's why, as a new mom, exercising with baby as much as you can makes sense, as does fitting in activity that gets you moving while you go about your mom duties.

The *Lean Mommy* plan features progressive routines that gradually build up to longer, harder, and more frequent workouts.

YOUR ABS

Every mom is anxious to get their abs back into shape. This requires a combination of cardio to burn enough calories to reduce fat, and strengthening exercises to tone up the weakened muscles.

Doing hundreds of sit-ups, crunches, or extreme leg-lifting Pilates ab moves is not the solution. It's ineffective to pummel away at your abs with exercises that will increase the spinal load on your lower back. Instead, you need to do less bending and more stabilizing. Learn to engage all the ab and back muscles that encircle your entire torso, known as the core, not only when you are exercising but through everyday mommy movements—picking up baby, driving the car, or using the bathroom. The first step is learning how to consciously contract these muscles. The following visualizations will help you focus on these muscles so that you can engage your core.

BELLY LACING

Your rib cage widens during pregnancy. Engaging your core muscles can help compress it afterward. Imagine that you have ribbon laced throughout the front, sides, and back of your rib cage. Imagine pulling the ends of the ribbon together so that your rib cage narrows. If you find this contraction difficult to intitiate, practice and visualize; your mind and the muscle will eventually connect.

CINCH THE CORSET

Going back to the ribbon image, imagine you are wearing an old-fashioned corset. Tighten that corset to bring in your entire waistline—the front, back, and sides. Do this with your muscles, not by holding your breath. Breathe (even if shallowly) through all of these exercises.

BUTTON YOUR BELLY BUTTON

Imagine you are wearing a very tight pair of jeans, the kind where you have to suck it all in to get them on. Now imagine that the button is broken. You need to button in your belly button or your pants will open up (quite embarrassing). Keep those jeans zipped up and buttoned up, again without holding your breath.

HEEL SLIDE

Lie on your back with your knees bent. Draw in your abdominals without holding your breath. Slowly slide one heel away from your body without changing the natural arch in your back. Your hips should not tilt. Extend your leg as far as you can without changing the position of your hips and lower back. When you find your end position, bring the heel back to starting position. Your abdominals should stay contracted throughout the movement. Repeat on the other side. This exercise can be done daily to regain strength at the core.

diastasis recti

You may have noticed a separation of the center of your abdomen during pregnancy. Diastasis recti occurs when your growing belly splits the connective tissue of the rectus abdominis muscle. Not sure if you have a diastasis? Lie on your back with your legs bent and feet flat on the floor. Place two fingers under your belly button and point them toward your toes. Contract your belly and curl up a few inches as if you were doing a crunch. If you can feel a large ridge when you wiggle your fingers down into your flesh, you have a diastasis. A normal separation is somewhere between one and two fingers. But a wider gap can cause problems. It shouldn't worsen after the baby is born, but without specific movements to help heal the separation, it won't improve. If you think you have a diastasis, see your doctor.

If you do have this separation, avoid doing exercises that pull on the stomach, such as twisting motions and oblique crunches, or any moves that appear to make your tummy bulge. Start with exercises that focus on your deepest core muscles. Try using a towel wrapped around your waistline to help cinch it together while performing abdominal exercises (as below).

SPLINTED CRUNCH

Lie on your back on top of a towel or scarf. Wrap the ends around your belly so that you are in effect cinching your waist together. With your feet flat and legs bent, draw in your abdominals without holding your breath. Do a small crunch by lifting your head and shoulders, but be sure to draw in your abs a little deeper as you raise up. If your abdominals poof out, you are lifting your head and shoulders too high. Repeat, raising up only to the point just *before* you see your abs bulge.

YOUR BACK

For every mom with weak, overstretched abs, there is a mom with an achy back. And if it doesn't hurt now, don't think you're in the clear. A recent study found that picking up objects while holding a baby in a front-pack carrier significantly increases the stress on the back. Even without a baby, repetitive back-bending moves are a recipe for back strain. All the mom-specific leaning over that you do, including picking up, putting down, and slumping over to nurse, can wreak real havoc on your back. Though you can't not perform many of these actions, the following muscle and body alignment tips can reduce strain during those stressful moments:

MAINTAIN YOUR SPINE'S NATURAL CURVE

The vertebrae that make up your spine do not form a perfectly vertical line. They are stacked in a slight S-shaped curve. Poor posture will distort some areas of the curve. Your spine is actually strongest when it is held in a position that maintains its natural curve, known as its neutral alignment.

Some women learn from old-fashioned fitness or dance classes that it's a good idea to flatten out the lower back curve, either when lying down and flattening the back to the floor, or when standing and tucking the hips under. In fact, this flexes, or bends, the spine, and puts more, not less, strain on your back. Your lower back is stronger and better able to handle excess loads if you move or lift things while your spine is in neutral position.

In practical terms, this means that when you lie on your back, you should try to maintain the curve so that there is a gap between the floor and your lower back. You can even place a small rolled-up towel in the space between the floor and the small of your back to support the position. When you are standing or performing an exercise, lengthen your spine so that you do not slump, and push your tailbone back slightly, rather than under. Every body has different ranges of motion so you may have to move your hips forward and back to locate the middle zone, or what position is neutral for your body. When you are sitting, placing a small pillow, rolled-up towel, or lumbar support at the base of your spine helps maintain a neutral position.

ENGAGE YOUR CORE MUSCLES

If you can consciously engage your core muscles most of the time—and especially before a moment of heavy exertion—you provide support to your spine. I have to remind myself all the time to brace and contract my abs. Try to catch yourself as much as possible and if you notice that your abs are pooched out, perform the visualizations above: Cinch the corset or button up your belly button. The more you do it, the more natural it will become. This will play a key role in helping you to protect your spine and to flatten your tummy.

One of the most stressful positions for your spine is to bend forward, twist, and try to lift something. And that's exactly what you do when you move the car seat or stroller in and out of your car! Here are some tips to make it easier:

- Avoid executing this bending maneuver while baby is sitting in the seat. Always move each separately to lighten the load.
- Start by bracing your entire torso before you move.
- Before bending forward, align your spine so that you are preserving its natural curve. Then, engage your core muscles to maintain that curve.
- Try hard to minimize the amount of bending at the lower back. Bend your knees to lower your body. Try a split-leg, lungelike stance and shift your body weight toward your front leg to *lean* your whole body forward more than bending just at the waist.
- Focus on bending and straightening your elbows to use your biceps to lift and lower.
- Take the same precautions when lowering and lifting anything heavy.

ESSENTIAL BACK PROTECTION

- Squat whenever you pick up baby or put him down. Never just lean over, bending at the lower back, if you can help it.
- Avoid holding baby hoisted on your hip. You'll shift your weight to one side to balance and that's just another stressful bending position for your spine. Instead, hold baby centered on your body whenever possible.
- A front-pack carrier is a wonderful way to be hands-free, and it helps centralize the baby load. But you can still distort your posture from the front placement of the baby. Anytime you wear baby in a front-pack carrier, keep your core strong and your spine in neutral. And definitely keep those shoulders pulled back!

> "I moved to a new community with a four-year-old and twenty-one-month-old triplets. I had no friends so I joined Stroller Strides and started pushing my four kids up hills. I met a group of moms and we now all train together for 5K and 10K races."
>
> —**KELLY MORSE, 40,**
> mom of Jason, 6, Cooper,
> Lukas, and Ruby, 3,
> Canyon Hills, California

- When you walk with the stroller, try not to hunch over it. Stand tall and lead with your chest.
- When you are moving baby or the seat, hold him close to your body.
- When you are nursing, bring baby to you instead of bending forward. Use a nursing pillow so that you can sit up straight.
- A lumbar support or pillow placed at your lower back in a chair helps you maintain your spine's natural lumbar curve as you sit. Sit tall, lifting up from, rather than sinking down into, your lower back.
- Even though you're happy to get off your tired feet, sitting bends the spine and can be more stressful for your back than standing. Try to avoid prolonged periods of sitting.
- When you are moving the baby in and out of the crib, always lower the rail.
- When you are setting baby down in a crib, high chair, or anywhere else, position yourself to do this without twisting your

back. Stand directly in front of where you are placing your child.

- Strengthening the muscles surrounding your shoulders and upper back, and stretching out tight chest muscles, will help maintain good posture. The *Lean Mommy* workouts include exercises to meet this need.

YOUR PELVIC FLOOR

If you've been wetting your pants lately, don't be ashamed! This is a common occurrence in new moms; studies show that nearly half experience it when they start exercising. The muscles at the base of your pelvis may have weakened during pregnancy. And the heavy load bearing down on your bladder may have led to stress incontinence. You may notice accidental urine leakage when you bend over

mommy meditation #2

Sit in a quiet upright position. Breathe quietly and notice the flow of air coming in and out of your nose. As you inhale, direct the air to the base of your spine. Imagine that the oxygen is lighting up the area so that you can see the lower half of your spine glowing a fiery red. Mentally shift your perspective so that you visualize the red at the end of your spine as if you were looking down a glass tube. With every inhalation, feel the red glow get brighter. Continue to exhale and feel the red flame grow so that it rises up your spine a little with each deep breath in. As it inches up, see a different color ignite. See and feel the purest hues of green, blue, orange, yellow, and purple all along your back. Continue seeing this rainbow until the colors rise from your neck to the top of your head. Form the colors into a beautiful rainbow with each subsequent breath. When you need energy, conjure up this picture of vibrant energy emanating from your spine.

or jump. Or you may feel a need to pee but without producing much fluid when you do (known as urge incontinence). Or you may be experiencing a mix of both symptoms.

There are differing levels of severity, but it is important to nip this problem in the bud now. Your risk of incontinence later in life is greatly increased the longer you experience postpartum incontinence. There are many causes of incontinence, and not all of them can be solved with pelvic floor exercises. But for many new moms, doing pelvic floor strengthening moves will reduce or cure incontinence.

Arnold Kegel, a gynecologist in the 1950s, conducted research on women with incontinence and found that pelvic floor strengthening exercises helped improve their condition. Since then, these exercises have been known as Kegel exercises. There are many ways to do them and, once you get the hang of it, you can do them anytime. Since you're squeezing internal muscles, no one can tell that you are doing them! Dr. Kegel also found that some of his research subjects experienced orgasms for the first time in their lives as a result of this pelvic floor conditioning. So, in addition to alleviating your bladder control issues, you may experience a bonus—enhanced sexual functioning! (Next baby, coming up!) Need more reasons why you should do these exercises? I didn't think so. Here's what you need to do:

1. You may have read somewhere that you should try to stop your urine flow while urinating to exercise these muscles. This is okay to try as a test to identify where the muscles are. But it's not a good idea to do this on a regular basis. Interrupting your flow may disrupt the way different pelvic floor muscles interact and the contractions may irritate your urethra. Instead, concentrate on the main pelvic floor muscles known as the levator ani group, with the main one being the pubococcygeus, near the vaginal entrance.

2. Start by clenching your butt, or your glutes, while standing, sitting, or lying on your back. Then, bring your mental focus inward from your butt squeeze to your anus. See if you can contract your anus. Then contract the muscles around your vaginal opening; I'm giving you the back end version first since many women are more familiar with clenching that area. Once you have it, change focus and emphasize the contraction around your vaginal opening.

3. Practice makes perfect. If you did not do this exercise during pregnancy or your muscles were traumatized from a vaginal delivery, the muscle fibers will be weak, making it difficult to consciously contract these muscles at first. The good news is that these muscle fibers seem to heal fast, and by practicing a few times you will master the technique. (You can ask your gynecologist to show you how: He or she will insert her finger to ensure that you are doing it properly. You can do this yourself, too.)

4. Once you can properly execute this exercise, squeeze in these three different ways to train all the muscle fibers effectively:

   First, simply hold the squeeze without letting go for as long as you can. At first, you might only be able to hold it for three seconds! Work up to ten seconds or longer. Don't hold your breath—just breathe normally.

   Second, squeeze hard and then completely relax. Turn some music on, and practice squeezing to the beat. Again, breathe normally. Work your way up to twenty repetitions.

   Third, speed up the contractions—do a lighter but faster squeeze-release.

5. There are many methods of pelvic floor training and research has not yet pinpointed the perfect way. If you do

them at all, it's a good thing. Various products are available on the market to help you strengthen these muscles including vaginal cones, little tamponlike dumbbells that you insert before walking around (in your house, not on the street!). Your pelvic floor gets an extra resistance challenge by preventing them from falling out.

OTHER OUCH SPOTS

Although ab and back problems are the obvious trouble spots, you may also aggravate other areas as well:

YOUR WRISTS: Many moms experience carpal tunnel syndrome due to swelling in the wrists. All that picking up, putting down, and lugging around means that your hands are constantly working. It's easy to flex your wrist too much while carrying a heavy load. So when lifting, check to see that each wrist is straight and in line with your forearm. Try not to bend them to pick something up.

"AFTER six months I am back to the weight I was before I had my two kids and my arms are more toned than ever before, even after being on bed rest with my second son."

—TAO MORAN-SCHIFMAN, 37,
mom of Ethan, 4, and Adin, 2,
Bronx, New York

YOUR SHOULDER GIRDLE: Many moms complain of stabbing pain deep underneath, or in the back of, their shoulders. This pain may be caused from overstretching of the shoulder muscles when your shoulder blades separate as you hold your baby, and from changes in posture, the added weight of heavier breasts, and shortened chest muscles. To alleviate this pain, focus on keeping your shoulders back and down while holding baby, and hold baby on both sides of your body, switching sides frequently. The external rotator cuff exercise on pages 138–139 will help strengthen weakened shoulder muscles.

YOUR FEET: Most moms find that their feet spread during pregnancy, even gaining a size. Swelling from pregnancy and labor can keep feet feeling painful and uncomfortable even after having a baby. Do ankle circles and stretches regularly to keep blood flowing and make sure you are not squeezing into too-tight shoes.

SI PAIN: This is pain near the two small dimples at the back of your lower spine. The sacroiliac joint is located at the point where the lower spine meets the pelvis. It is not normally a movable joint, but it can separate during pregnancy or labor. Bending, lifting, and carrying can exacerbate this problem. Avoid any exercises that increase stress to this area and check with your doctor if you are experiencing this pain.

DEAL WITH DISCOMFORT

You're simply not going to stick with exercise if it makes you feel bad!

- If exercise is uncomfortable for your nursing breasts, layer two compressive or sports bras and hold your crossed arms over your chest for any bouncing, jumping, or running moves.
- Wait until breast abscesses or mastitis are healed before starting workouts.
- If your belly feels like it is sagging rather than supporting your spine, wear a support belt or tights the first few weeks of workouts.
- Nurse just before exercise so your breasts will feel less full.
- If your baby fusses at the breast after you exercise, wipe it with a clean wet towel. He or she may not like the taste of sweat.
- When incontinence catches you off guard during a workout:
  - Avoid jumping, running, or bending forward (and that includes bending ab moves). Stick to low-impact activity.
  - Next, concentrate on learning how to squeeze your pelvic floor (detailed on pages 63–65) along with your core to provide some support.

- Avoid drinking caffeine at least two hours prior to exercise.
- Wear a pad. Choose one with a lower level of protection if you find you're uncomfortable with a maxi.

TOP 5 WAYS TO STICK TO EXERCISE

HAVE FUN!

If the only way to exercise was to drop everything for a solid hour of exercise, I probably wouldn't do it very often. Keeping it short and making it fun helps make it easier to squeeze in. If you are a former gym rat to whom nothing but a solid hour or two counts as a workout, realize that your workout doesn't have to fit a traditional forty-five-minute routine. My exercise now is usually playing with my kids, or meeting other moms for a walk, or a Stroller Strides class. When I can fit it in, I go on a relaxing, long run, but often it's too hard to take the time. You can still burn a lot of calories from walking the dog twice a day, or playing with your kids by kicking and throwing a ball and playing tag.

BE FLEXIBLE

Find a way to fit activity into your lifestyle, no matter what. I rarely have time to go to the gym anymore. So I go running straight from my front door. I've even popped a few exercise videos or DVDs into the video player.

GET UP EARLIER

It's always a toss-up: Should you get up earlier and sacrifice precious sleep to squeeze in a workout, or will you benefit more from the extra ZZZ? It depends upon the amount of sleep deprivation you are experiencing. Research indicates that getting less sleep than you need may lead to weight gain. On the other hand, if it's a mere half an hour less and you wake up to rev up for a workout, you may get an

"MY daughter, Leslie, had colic and cried nonstop for fifteen months, so we stayed captive in the house. I not only got mushy but I lost contact with my friends. We then changed towns and I found Stroller Strides. Stroller Strides helped me not only to work out but to make friends, and once Leslie started feeling better, for her to make friends, too. I now have a healthier, happier family."

—CHRISTINA LAMBERT, 30,

mom of Leslie, 2,
Glen Allen, Virginia

energy boost and extra calorie burn that may cancel out that effect. Shortly after my son started sleeping through the night, I realized that getting up before the rest of the family at 5:00 a.m. was beneficial. Having one hour to myself was a gift so great that for me it was worth losing sleep.

MEET A FRIEND (OR FRIENDS)

Working out with a partner not only helps the time pass more quickly, but when you have to cancel or don't show, your friend will hold you accountable. Whether you miss the socializing or you feel guilty for letting your friend down, that may be what keeps you going back the next time! This is a large reason for the success that women have with Stroller Strides. The number of women that still attend four years after they join is extremely high, and much more than with traditional exercise programs. Why? Because these women form friendships and have fun working out together and with their kids. It's double-duty: a playgroup and time with the girls.

CROSS-TRAIN

Mixing up what you do is always a good idea. And experienced exercisers often get a real boost in motivation when they simply try something new (while beginners are still getting the hang of things). If you are in a slump and trying to forge past a plateau, a new activity is often just the challenge that your body needs. So whether you try a yoga video, start skating, or start playing catch with your husband, keep variety into your routine. Read Martica's book, *Cross-Training for Dummies*, for more tips.

Signing up for a race or a fun run, enrolling in salsa lessons, or joining a team is a great way to make yourself stick to a longer-term plan. If you're working toward something specific, you have to go through all the steps to get to the goal. I usually sign up for half-marathons because I know that if I make that commitment, I'll *have* to get my runs in!

Now you're ready to start the *Lean Mommy* plan.

CHAPTER **6**

The *Lean Mommy* Plan

You're ready to start the first day of the *Lean Mommy* plan. This program is designed to help you integrate smart eating and exercise habits into your current lifestyle. Follow my simple cognitive and behavior change recommendations each week and you'll soon find yourself thinking and acting in more positive, healthy ways.

HOW TO FOLLOW THE PLAN

I've outlined two plans, based on fitness levels. Choose the one that best describes your status *now.* Each plan is divided into three progressive phases. Follow the prescription in each phase, and stick to each phase for six to eight weeks. Generally, that's about the amount of time it takes for your cardiovascular and muscular systems to adapt to a period of regular exercise and to show measurable results.

That's not to say that you might not see progress sooner—you probably will. Each time you work out, you experience immediate benefits. You may notice a mood boost, or increases in stamina and energy. After just a few sessions, you may become aware that you don't fatigue as easily. And there are short-term physiological adaptations that you might not even notice: a boost in your good cholesterol (HDL), or an improvement in the way your body metabolizes fat. But noticeable weight changes, fat loss, or increases in strength may take at least a couple of months to attain.

If you are irregular with your workouts, or find that they continue to be challenging, you may want to extend the amount of time you spend in one phase.

Injuries are usually the result of doing too much too soon. The *Lean Mommy* plan is slow and progressive to prevent that from happening. Of course, if you twist your ankle getting out of bed, or your back is sore because you picked up baby in the stroller and a bag of groceries at the same time, you should hold off on any vigorous activities or exercises that aggravate your ailment. Any acute injury should be seen by a doctor or physical therapist immediately. Any minor ache or pain that persists for more than a couple of days should also be assessed by a medical professional.

You are ready to move up to the next phase when 1) the exercises or workouts start to feel too easy, 2) you feel bored, or 3) you notice that you are looking for excuses to skip sessions.

WHICH PLAN IS RIGHT FOR YOU?

If you are new to exercise or have not exercised regularly in more than six months, choose Plan 1 on page 78.

If you are an experienced exerciser or have already started being active again, choose Plan 2 on page 79. This plan is slightly more difficult than Plan 1. But it still starts you off slow and gradually builds to harder, longer, more frequent workouts. Remember, you may be weaker than you think after being pregnant and giving birth. You can't just jump back into the same workouts that you used to do. Use your best judgment. If you start a plan and it seems too challenging, then drop down to a lower intensity (fewer reps or sets, or less time). If it is too easy, then adjust upward accordingly.

Each plan provides a program of progressive cardio workouts and muscle-toning moves. It also includes weekly stretching, daily Kegels, and posture reminders, and a weekly tip on integrating a new behavior or eating strategy.

Remember, get your doctor's clearance before starting Lean Mommy *or any other exercise program.*

THE CARDIO MOVES

We have provided you with physical activity guidelines. These start slow and short, and gradually build up to longer periods. You can accumulate these calorie-burning minutes in different ways and at different intensities: playing with your kids, doing a more traditional cardio workout, walking or running with the stroller or on your own.

Although any amount of activity is good for your health, those who see dramatic changes in their body do so after being committed to exercising for at least three and up to six times a week. But if you are a beginner, this doesn't mean that you should overdo it. Even lifestyle activities (playing with your kids, for instance) will count. You will start with three days and build up to longer and more frequent sessions. When you reach the upper end of the spectrum, cross-train and incorporate several types of cardio and lifestyle activity into your week. This can keep you motivated and help reduce injury resulting from repetitive stress.

THE MUSCLE-STRENGTHENING MOVES

For each plan, I've provided three different workouts to choose from. If you want to head outdoors, do the Stroller Workout. If you are strapped for time, pull out rubber tubing for the Mom-Has-Just-a-

Minute Workout, which you can do at home, in your backyard, or while visiting grandma and grandpa across town or across the country. And when you are looking for an energetic way to bond with baby, do the Baby Weight Workout. No equipment—except baby—needed! You can do it virtually anywhere. All workouts target your major muscles, including those that specifically need strengthening after childbirth, to help you meet the demands of motherhood. Include one, two, or all three workouts in your weekly regimen.

For each workout, perform each exercise shown. Some exercises have optional moves that target the same muscle group. If a move is designated as an advanced option, wait until you feel fit enough to do it. If you feel weak or wobbly doing the first option, don't move on until you can execute the first exercise with complete control.

You can use dumbbells with most of these exercises. But I've chosen to use resistance rubber tubing (which can be purchased online at any sporting goods store or through www.strollerstrides .com). It's easy to use, lightweight, fits easily into your stroller or diaper bag, and works out all body parts. The Baby Weight Workout uses baby as your resistance. And just as you progress to heavier dumbbells or stronger tubes, you'll naturally increase your resistance (and strength) as baby grows bigger!

If you have diastasis recti, avoid doing the ab exercises suggested. Instead, do those described on page 93.

USING RUBBER TUBING

Pumping rubber is like pumping iron. You'll feel the same fatigue if you lift a weight around twelve times as you do with the same exercise using a tube—you've worked using the same relative amount of resistance. In other words, just because you're using tubes doesn't mean that you are getting an easier workout!

The difference is in the mechanics of the tools. While weights are gravity-based, the tubing's resistance comes from its elastic properties—the rubber provides resistance when you pull it.

You can use any brand of tubing or tubes. I prefer the sturdy tubing with handles because it is easier to grip. You can adjust the toughness of your workout with various tubes of varying strengths, usually differentiated by color. Generally, the shorter and/or thicker a tube is, the tougher the resistance.

To figure out what size tube is right for you, try various sizes until you find one that makes you feel fatigued by the end of one set of exercises. Different moves may require different-sized tubes, depending upon the strength of the particular muscle group you are targeting.

CHANGING INTENSITY WITH AN EXERCISE TUBE

You can make an exercise harder or easier in several ways:

- Use different sizes of tubes.
- Shorten the tube to make it harder or lengthen the tube to make it easier (i.e., wrap tube around your hand once or twice, or grip it closer or farther from middle).
- Move both arms at the same time instead of one at a time.
- When performing an exercise that involves standing on the tube, stand with one or both feet to adjust the tension.
- Add balance to an exercise by lifting up one foot. Adding balance triggers more action from your core muscles to hold yourself steady.

> ### SAFETY FIRST!
>
> - Inspect exercise tubing before each use for worn spots, nicks, or tears. Discontinue use if damaged.
> - For exercises that require you to attach tubing to something stable, use only a sturdy pole, beam, or fence. NEVER use the stroller or a chair.
> - Avoid exposing tubing to extreme heat or cold; never leave it in water or direct sunlight.
> - Avoid using tubing on rough or abrasive surfaces.
> - Never pull tubing directly toward your face.
> - Never pull tubing in the direction of your child.
> - Never stretch exercise tubing more than three times its length. (If you can stretch the tube this far, you need a heavier-strength tube.)
> - A tube can break at any time while you use it. So use good judgment when exercising around baby, and be cautious if you are carrying baby in a front-pack carrier.

MOMMY MOVES

To bond and make the workout fun for baby, I've designed ways to incorporate songs and baby activity into your workout. The developmental needs of a newborn are different from those of a toddler. Brand-new babies are enthralled simply being outdoors. As baby gets older, incorporate special toys like bubbles, music, and activities. Many of us at Stroller Strides have special toy bags filled with toys, mini-games, and books that are to be used only during our stroller walks. That way, these toys stay special and your little one looks forward to your workout.

You don't have to sing to baby at every station, but I've provided song suggestions to keep it fun—feel free to use your own! (You may feel silly, but you'll be delightfully surprised when your baby starts to associate your workout time with his fun.) You can also use the tune to add a new challenge to your workout. For example, when you hit a pause in the music while singing nursery rhymes, freeze and hold the position you are in at that second. Or add a burst of cardio such as a jumping jack or march in place for a few seconds.

THE EATING PRESCRIPTION

You will be not be dieting on the *Lean Mommy* plan. You will simply be improving what you already eat. The eating portion of the *Lean Mommy* plan consists of you choosing better-quality foods. See Chapter 11, "What You Eat." But you also need to improve your eating behaviors. Review your Food and Fitness Diary. Then implement some of the suggestions in Chapter 12, "How to Eat," to revamp your current way of eating without changing it too drastically. For example, are there nonnutritious foods or drinks that you have daily or nearly every day that you could live without? If you have two cups of coffee every day with two sugars each, can you adjust to a slightly less sweet taste by dropping down to one sugar each and save thirty calories every day? Each week, make a small and simple change toward better health. Do not do anything drastic where you leave yourself feeling deprived; just make better choices. Before you know it, those little changes will add up and you will find yourself eating leaner and more healthfully than ever before!

THE KEGELS

A key part of your recovery is rehabbing your pelvic floor. Kegels should be part of a woman's life at all times, even long after childbirth. All women should strengthen their pelvic floor muscles. Follow the prescription accompanying each phase.

THE LEAN MOMMY PLAN

PHYSICAL ACTIVITY: You can include low-intensity lifestyle activities like playing with the kids or walking during errands. Also include moderate-intensity cardio activities such as walking or running with your stroller.

MUSCLE MOVES: Follow all three workouts each week: the Stroller Workout, the Baby Weight Workout, and the Mom-Has-Just-a-Minute Workout. Do recommended sets and reps, unless otherwise indicated within a specific exercise.

FLEXIBILITY: Follow the Stretching Workout, or you can also do stretching on your own.

KEGELS: Include daily pelvic floor exercises. You can do them anytime, and even split them up during the day, as long as you fit them in.

POSTURE PICKUP: Focus on strengthening your core muscles and maintaining good spinal alignment during mommy moments throughout your day. Choose exercises from Chapter 9, "The Mom-Has-Just-a-Minute Workout," as suggested.*

EATING HABIT: Review Chapters 11 and 12, "What You Eat," "How to Eat." Focus on adopting one improvement to your normal eating behavior as suggested each week.*

You may integrate each component of the plan together, or do

---

*Post your daily or weekly Posture Pickup and Eating Habit on a sticky note around the house as a reminder.

LEAN MOMMY PLAN 1 FOR BEGINNERS

If you are new to exercise or have not exercised regularly in more than six months

ACTIVITY	PHASE 1	PHASE 2	PHASE 3
Physical Activity	3–4 sessons a week at least 10–30 minutes per session	4–5 sessions a week for 25–45 minutes per session per day	5–6 sessions a week for 40–60 minutes per session
Muscle Moves	2 sessions a week Do 1 set of 15 repetitions of each exercise from chosen workout	3 sessions a week Do 2 sets of 15 repetitions of each exercise from chosen workout	3 sessions a week Do 3 sets of 12 repetitions of each exercise from chosen workout (progress to stronger band if needed)
Flexibility	At least 1 session a week Hold each stretch 10–30 seconds	At least 1 session a week Hold each stretch 10–30 seconds	At least 1 session a week Hold each stretch 10–30 seconds
Kegels	Daily • Hold one contraction for 3–5 seconds, 5 reps • Quickly contract-release for 10 reps	Daily • Hold one contraction for 5–10 seconds, 5–10 reps • Quickly contract-release for 15–20 reps	Daily • Hold one contraction for 10 seconds, 15–20 reps • Quickly contract-release for 20–30 reps
Eating Habit	Daily Aim for eating 5 healthful meals and snacks, spread evenly throughout the day	Daily Choose from the Good Dining Habits in Chapter 12 and follow a different one each week	Daily Try one nutritious new item from Super Foods for New Moms in Chapter 11
Posture Pickup	Daily Choose one core-strengthening move from Your Abs in Chapter 5 to do throughout your busy day each week	Daily Choose a different Mommy Move every day to emphasize each week from Essential Back Protection in Chapter 5	Daily Choose a different Mommy Move every day to emphasize each week from Essential Back Protection in Chapter 5

LEAN MOMMY PLAN 2 FOR EXPERIENCED EXERCISERS

If you are an experienced exerciser or have already started being active again

ACTIVITY	PHASE 1	PHASE 2	PHASE 3
Physical Activity	3–5 sessions a week for 20–30 minutes per session	5 sessions a week for 35–45 minutes per session	5–6 sessions a week for 45–60 minutes per session
Muscle Moves	3 sessions a week Do 2 sets of 12 repetitions of each exercise from chosen workout	3 sessions a week Do 3 sets of 12 repetitions of each exercise from chosen workout	3 sessions a week Do 3 sets of 10 repetitions of each exercise from chosen workout (progress to stronger band if needed)
Flexibility	At least 1 session a week Hold each stretch 10–30 seconds	At least 1 session a week Hold each stretch 10–30 seconds	At least 1 session a week Hold each stretch 10–30 seconds
Kegels	Daily • Hold one contraction for 3–10 seconds, 5–10 reps • Quickly contract-release for 10 reps	Daily • Hold one contraction for 10–15 seconds, 10–15 reps • Quickly contract-release for 15–25 reps	Daily • Hold one contraction for 10–20 seconds, 15–25 reps • Quickly contract-release for 30–50 reps
Eating Habit	Daily Aim for eating 5 healthful meals and snacks, spread evenly throughout the day	Daily Choose from the Good Dining Habits in Chapter 12 and follow a different one each week	Daily Choose one nutritious new food in Super Foods for New Moms in Chapter 11
Posture Pickup	Daily Choose one core-strengthening move from Your Abs in Chapter 5 to do throughout your busy day each week.	Daily Choose a different Mommy Move every day to emphasize each week from Essential Back Protection in Chapter 5	Daily Choose a different Mommy Move every day to emphasize each week from Essential Back Protection in Chapter 5

them separately. It's not so important how you fit your *Lean Mommy* moves in, just make sure to do them! For example:

- Within one session, mix your Muscle Moves workout within your Physical Activity minutes (i.e., perform band moves in between strolling).
- Do the Physical Activity minutes in the morning, and the Muscle Moves followed by your Flexibility workout in the afternoon.
- Break up your Physical Activity minutes (if you are aiming for 45 minutes, for example, do 15 in the morning on a cardio machine and then play tag with the kids for 30 minutes).

CHAPTER **7**

The Stroller Workout

By this point, you're ready for a breath of fresh air—and this is the perfect workout for that. That's because you'll be buckling baby into the stroller for a ride outdoors. Exposure to daylight and connecting with nature can provide you both with a much needed mood boost. Plus, it stimulates production of vitamin D in both you and baby. So on days when you need a breather, strap in little one and head for the hills (or the park, or playground). Weather not good? Go to the shopping mall.

WORKING OUT WITH BABY AND A STROLLER

You can get a cardio workout that burns lots of calories by picking up the pace from a slow walk to a brisk stroll with your stroller. In this workout, you will re-create your own gym outdoors, using benches and fences along with your rubber tubing and the stroller for balance.

Any stroller will work, with the exception of an umbrella stroller (these are not designed for stability or speed). It's easiest to work out with a jogging stroller, which steers more easily and allows you to maintain better posture. I've designed the Stroller Strides Fitness Stroller by BOB. It's made not only for intense strolling, but is equipped with a fitness kit that includes tubing for resistance exercises. Whichever stroller you choose, make sure that the wheels and construction are solid, and that baby is comfortably strapped in.

The beauty about being outside is that your child is happily distracted—and for a moment, you're off the hook from entertaining duties. Babies under one year are absolutely fascinated with leaves blowing on a tree and clouds moving through the sky. That's not to say that you aren't fun to watch: In our Stroller Strides classes, the kids love seeing their mommies do silly things!

I recommend that you do this workout in intervals to keep your child stimulated. So move with the stroller, walking or running, then stop every few minutes and do one or two exercises with your tube.

When you are doing your exercises, turn baby to look at a busy playground, scenic park, rushing pedestrians, or whatever catches his or her fancy. Or face baby and keep up the rapport as you whip through your routine by singing songs. Research shows that you can teach toddlers new words through songs. (You may not think you are the greatest crooner in the world, but your baby sure loves your voice!)

If your baby isn't crazy about being in the stroller, be patient and firm. Do what feels right, but keep in mind that if you take him out every time he whines, he'll learn that crying is the key to getting out. Stick to a regular schedule of specific days and times when you use the stroller. Baby will soon realize, Mom takes care of me all day long and this is the one hour I'm going to stay put here. If you know your baby is comfortable and not hungry, don't feel guilty

SAFETY FIRST

- When you park your stroller, be aware of cars, bikes, skaters, Frisbees, balls, or dogs!
- Always stay within one hand's reach away from your stroller.
- Always lock the brake whenever you are performing movements around the stroller.
- Carry plenty of fluids for both you and baby, especially on hot days.
- Don't forget to apply sunblock on your baby if she's over six months. If not, keep her well shaded.
- Always buckle baby in. Some moms feel that they don't need to strap in the baby because she isn't moving yet and can't get out. Wrong! If someone bumps into your stroller and knocks it over, you want baby secure.

WHAT TO LOOK FOR IN A STROLLER

Many moms have a fleet of strollers for different activities. It's easier to use just one, but it must suit all your needs. I use my Stroller Strides Fitness Stroller for everything, from exercising to trips to the mall. Since it has an infant car seat attachment, I've used it since my baby was very small. Some strollers are better than others for working out. Since this is your most used baby item, it's important to get one with the most helpful features. Look for these things:

REVOLVING FRONT WHEEL: A static wheel is great if you're moving in a straight line. But if not, you have to lift the back wheels to turn. Swivel wheels strain wrists less because you can turn the stroller with one hand. A good model also has wheels that lock.

ADJUSTING CANOPY: Most strollers have canopies, but many are not fully adjustable. Depending on the position of the sun, you'll want to be able to pull the canopy partially or all the way down.

PADDED HARNESS: For baby to have a comfortable, enjoyable experience, look for padded straps. You can add a snuggly insert to make it even cushier for him.

ADJUSTABLE HANDLES OR APPROPRIATE HEIGHT: Your stroller should allow you to walk with good posture, and not cause you to hunch over or reach forward uncomfortably. If you're very short or very tall, your options may be limited.

LOTS OF STORAGE: Moms carry a lot of stuff. Make sure there are ample compartments for diapers, spare clothes, and so on, as well as a console to hold water, keys, and exercise tubes.

SHOCKS: There has recently been concern that a baby may get Shaken Baby Syndrome (SBS) from bouncing in the stroller. SBS is a term that describes symptoms of brain injury that may occur from the impact of shaking a baby or small child. Choose a model with shock absorbers to keep the ride smooth.

BRAKE: Look for strong brakes. Many moms prop their strollers against something to keep them from rolling. You wouldn't drive a car with bad brakes, and you shouldn't drive a stroller with bad brakes. A foot brake is more dependable than a handlebar brake.

WHEELS: The kind of wheels you need depends on the kind of terrain you'll be covering. Most likely this will vary from rolling on a smooth sidewalk to dirt. A tire with tread better handles all terrains. A no-tread tire is better for flat, smooth roads.

Now that you've picked out the right stroller, you're ready to roll!

about keeping him in the stroller for a short time. I've seen hundreds of kids each day in our classes. Most babies love the workouts with mom. For those who fuss, the moms who stick it out and keep baby in the stroller soon have happy babies joining us.

1A. STROLLER SQUAT

BODY BONUS: Helps get your bottom back to its pre-baby state by firming up your glutes.

START: Stand behind your stroller so that your arms are shoulder-width apart, with your hands resting on the handlebars, legs hip-width apart, feet and knees facing forward. Stand tall and engage your abs.

FINISH: Bear body weight in your heels as you inhale and lower body. Push your hips back behind you so upper body leans forward. Stop when knees bend to 90 degrees and keep calves perpendicular to the ground. Pause, then exhale and contract glutes to straighten legs and return to standing. Repeat.

TECHNIQUE TIP: Decrease pressure on knees by keeping them directly above the ankles, instead of forward past toes. Rather than dropping straight down, imagine someone pulling your hips back to the horizon. The stroller should enable you to get a little bit lower than without a stroller. I have one client who always says, "If you don't squeeze it, no one else will want to." So squeeze those glutes!

MOMMY MOVE: If baby is fussy, release brake, so baby rocks when you move. When you squat, pull the stroller back. When you come up, push it forward. Or, stand in front and play peekaboo or "this little piggy" with baby's feet as you squat without the stroller.

1B. STROLLER PLIÉ SQUAT (option to 1A)

BODY BONUS: Tightens your inner thighs and glutes.

START: Stand behind stroller and face handlebars. Open your legs in a straddle, feet set much wider than your shoulders, toes turned out, pointing to corners. Rest hands lightly on handlebars.

FINISH: Keeping back straight, bend knees and lower hips until legs and hips are bent around 90 degrees. Then exhale as you push your heels into the ground and squeeze glutes and inner thighs to return to standing. Repeat.

TECHNIQUE TIP: Avoid tucking pelvis under; maintain the natural curve in your lower back while tightening your abs. If your knees feel strained, spread feet wider and/or shift body weight slightly out in back as you lower.

ADVANCED OPTION: Pause at the bottom of the plié and lift your left heel. Pulse for 8 counts and then switch to right. Continue in 8, 4, 2 and then single pulses. Try holding the bottom of the plié while lifting both heels up.

MOMMY MOVE: To liven up the exercise, release brake. Hold the lowest point of plié, engage your core to stabilize, and push stroller back and forth to rock baby as you sing "I'm a little teapot."

1C. STROLLER BALLET BARRE (option to 1A)

BODY BONUS: Improves balance, tones your calves, and works your butt and thighs.

START: Stand behind the stroller and lightly grasp bar. Raise heels to balance on toes. Lower body as far as you can while keeping chest lifted and pelvis in neutral. Go down until your thighs say, "Yes, I feel it!"

FINISH: When you reach the lowest position, do small pulses contracting your glutes.

TECHNIQUE TIP: If your knees feel strained, avoid bending so low that you push your knees too far forward.

ADVANCED OPTION: Shift weight to one leg at a time as you lower, without shifting hips.

_____

MOMMY MOVE: Find a song that helps keep you slow and controlled. Customize songs to incorporate baby's name. Here's my version of "Little Miss Muffet."

Little Miss (your baby's name) / Little Mr. (for a boy)

Sat on a tuffet

Eating her/his curds and whey.

Along came a spider,

Who sat down beside him/her,

And Miss/Mr. (your baby's name) said, "Good day."

2A. STROLLER LUNGE

BODY BONUS: Firms up your butt and thighs.

START: Stand about two feet away from stroller. Extend arms in front, hands resting on handlebar. Spread legs in a split stance as far apart as you can comfortably, right leg in front of the left. Distribute most of your body weight between front heel and back toe (with back heel raised). Stand tall and tighten your torso.

FINISH: Inhale, and lower hips by bending both knees. Stop when front thigh is parallel to the ground. Pause, exhale, and squeeze glutes and thighs to return to straight-leg, starting position. Repeat, then switch legs. Make sure overall lunging motion glides up and down, rather than forward and back, to avoid stressing front knee. Keep upper body upright, shoulders down and back, chest lifted.

TECHNIQUE TIP: If you feel strain in back knee at the lowest part of lunge, try not to bend quite as much. Instead, step back foot a few inches farther back and lower with a straighter back leg. For a static lunge, keep brake on the stroller. If you want baby to keep moving, release brake and gently push and pull her as you lower and raise your body.

ADVANCED OPTION: Take a walking step forward and push the stroller forward with each lunge.

MOMMY MOVE: Move baby to a different position in his stroller or even hold him if he needs soothing and sing our version of "One, Two, Buckle My Shoe."

1, 2 Lunge like I do

3, 4 Let's do some more

5, 6 Let's have some kicks

7, 8 Don't lock your legs straight

9, 10 Let's do them again!

2B. STROLLER KNEE-LIFT LUNGE (OPTION TO 2A)

BODY BONUS: Improves balance while toning your glutes and thighs.

START: Stand about two feet away from stroller and extend arms, hands resting on handlebar. Start in a lunge stance, right leg in front of left. Bend front knee to lower hips until front thigh is parallel to floor and knee is bent to a 90 degree angle. Keep front knee over ankle. Raise back heel to distribute body weight between front heel and back toe.

FINISH: Exhale and contract butt as you move left foot forward, bringing it back toward your body, raising knee in front of you. Pause and balance on right leg, still lightly touching handles, when you reach standing. Then extend left foot back and lower into lunge again. Repeat, then switch legs.

TECHNIQUE TIP: Avoid letting lower back collapse as you raise knee in front; hold chest up and stand tall throughout move. Be careful not to collapse or hunch over stroller.

2C. STROLLER LUNGE EXTENSION (OPTION TO 2A)

BODY BONUS: Gives an extra boost to your glutes by strengthening your lower body.

START: Stand about two feet away from stroller and extend arms, hands on handlebar. Start in a lunge, right leg in front of left. Bend front knee to lower hips until front thigh is parallel to floor and knee is bent to 90 degree angle. Keep front calf perpendicular to ground. Distribute body weight between front heel and back toe (back heel raised).

FINISH: Squeeze glutes and front thigh to straighten legs and simultaneously lift left leg behind you about one foot from floor. Pause and squeeze left glute, then drop left foot and lower into lunge and repeat. Then switch legs.

TECHNIQUE TIP: Avoid overarching lower back as you extend leg. Engage your abs and move slowly, stopping when you feel a slight contraction in butt and lower back.

3. OUTDOOR ROW

BODY BONUS: Helps keep the lats and rhomboids in your back strong.

START: Loop tubing through a mesh fence at chest height. Hold each handle with palms facing down. Tube should be taut (step a few feet back to reduce any slack). Stand with feet hip-width apart and keep your knees soft.

FINISH: Tighten core muscles for stability. As you exhale, pull arms back, bending elbows out to sides at shoulder level. Stop when they reach your sides. Inhale and straighten arms, then repeat.

TECHNIQUE TIP: Try not to scrunch shoulders up to your ears. Hold them low throughout and focus on engaging all back muscles during move.

MOMMY MOVE: This one is a natural for doing along to "Row, Row, Row Your Boat."

4. OUTDOOR TUBE CURL

BODY BONUS: Buffs up your biceps.

START: Loop tube through a low part of mesh fence. Stand in front of fence and hold each handle with palms facing up. Step back until tube is taut.

FINISH: As you exhale, bend elbows and pull tube ends to raise hands toward shoulders. Hold, then lower and repeat.

TECHNIQUE TIP: Keep abs tight and hold upper arms close to body throughout move.

MOMMY MOVE: Move to our version of "He's Been Working on the Railroad."

Mommy's exercising outside,
On this special day

Mommy's exercising outside
Not just to pass the time away.
Don't you see me getting stronger,
Rise up so early in the morn!
Don't you see me getting stronger,
(Baby's name) toot your horn!

5A. OUTDOOR TRICEPS DIPS

BODY BONUS: Firms up backs of upper arms.

START: Sit on edge of a bench. Place hands on either side of body, fingers down. Scoot hips forward until rear end is in front of the bench seat.

FINISH: Inhale and lower hips by bending elbows to about 90 degrees. Pause, then exhale and straighten elbows to push up to the starting position. Repeat.

TECHNIQUE TIP: Avoid moving so deep that your upper arms move far past your shoulders' normal range of motion.

ADVANCED OPTION: Straighten legs instead of bending them for more intensity. Avoid this exercise if it exacerbates wrist pain or carpal tunnel syndrome. Do tubing option instead.

MOMMY MOVE: Baby can learn direction, counting, and tempo from your exercises. Since triceps dips use an up/down movement, call out "Up" and "Down." Baby will soon learn the concept and follow along.

5B. OUTDOOR TUBE TRICEPS PUSH-DOWN (OPTION TO 5A)

BODY BONUS: Firms up back of upper arms.

START: Loop tube through fence at face height. Hold on to each handle and step about two to three feet away from fence while facing it. Bend elbows, hold arms close to sides, palms facedown. Step back if tubes feel loose.

FINISH: Exhale and contract abs as you push hands straight down toward ground, pulling on tube to straighten elbows. Hold, then bend elbows to return to start and repeat.

TECHNIQUE TIP: Keep wrists neutral: perfectly straight and aligned with forearms.

MOMMY MOVE: Do this exercise to the tune of "Five Little Monkeys." At first, some of those monkeys might still stay on the bed as you might not have the stamina to finish the song. As you build up your strength, you'll be able to get all those monkeys off the bed!

6A. STROLLER PUSH-UP

BODY BONUS: Strengthens chest and core muscles.

START: Kneel in front of stroller facing baby. Place each hand on lower edge of stroller footrest or wheel base. Then walk your knees back until arms are fully extended and head, shoulders, hips, and knees form a diagonal line.

FINISH: Tighten your abs and bend elbows out to the sides to lower your chest to baby. Hold, then push back up to straight-arm position. Repeat.

TECHNIQUE TIP: Once you get stronger, balance on your toes, instead of knees, by extending legs straight out behind you. Keep hips neither piked pointing up to the ceiling, nor sagging toward the floor, but in a neutral position so body forms a diagonal line from head to toe.

- Make sure that stroller is stable before doing this exercise.
- Holding on to stroller on sides with wrists in neutral may be more comfortable. Skip this exercise if it aggravates your wrists.

MOMMY MOVE: Baby will enjoy this move because you are so close. You will usually get some giggles as you lower your body toward him! If you feel like a song, here's a greeting sung to "Good Morning to You":

Good morning to you,
Good morning to you,
Good morning dear (baby name),
Good morning to you!

6B. OUTDOOR TABLE PUSH-UPS (OPTION TO 6A)

BODY BONUS: Strengthens chest muscles and core ab muscles.

START: Find a sturdy table, place hands on edge of tabletop more than shoulder-width apart, fingers pointing forward. Take a few steps back and simultaneously lower hips so body forms a diagonal line from head to toe. Tighten abs.

FINISH: Bend elbows out to sides and lower chest toward table-top, maintaining rigid body alignment as you do. Then exhale and push hands down to straighten elbows and push up. Repeat.

TECHNIQUE TIP: Look down, not forward, to keep neck aligned with spine. Avoid this move if wrists are uncomfortable.

MOMMY MOVE: Do push-ups to a counting song such as "The Ants Go Marching One by One." See how far you get and add to song as you get stronger. At first you might only get to "The ants go marching two by two." As you get fitter those ants might end up marching by the dozen!

7. STROLLER (ISOMETRIC) CRUNCH

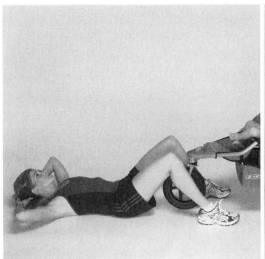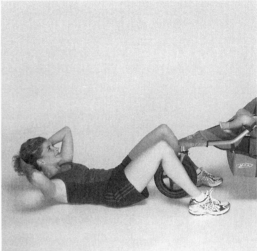

BODY BONUS: Firms up abs (and builds a strong core to protect your back).

START: Lie on your back in front of stroller, straddle front wheel with legs, and scoot close to baby. Bend knees and place feet flat on ground. Hold hands behind head, elbows bent out to sides. Do not flatten out the curve in your lower back. Instead, maintain the slight arch by tightening abs, without distorting the spine.

FINISH: Raise head, neck, and shoulders so shoulder blades just clear the ground, all the while maintaining the natural curve as much as possible. Rather than moving your body forward, hold the raised position without moving for 15 seconds, working up to 30 seconds. Lower and repeat.

TECHNIQUE TIP: Let head relax in your hands so as not to stress your neck.

MOMMY MOVE: Get a lightweight beach ball. Crunch and motion as if to hand ball to baby.

8. STROLLER REVERSE CURL

BODY BONUS: Targets six-pack with an emphasis on lower abs.

START: Lie in front of stroller with top of head next to front wheel. Bring both hands over your head to hold on to the wheel. Then bring both legs up above hips, with knees slightly bent.

FINISH: As you exhale, contract abs so hips tilt slightly forward, lower back rising slightly off ground. Hold, then slowly lower legs and repeat.

TECHNIQUE TIP: Keep movement subtle, focus on contracting abs, rather than using momentum to hike your back off the floor or to swing thighs. Keep abs and torso tightened.

———

MOMMY MOVE: Sing our version of "Mulberry Bush":

This is the way we work our tummies,
Work our tummies,
Work our tummies.
This is the way we work our tummies early in the morning.

9. STROLLER OBLIQUE CRUNCH

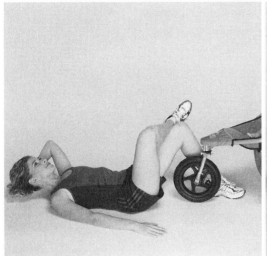 

BODY BONUS: Firms muscles that span waist.

START: Lie on back in front of stroller and straddle front wheel with legs to scoot close to baby. Cross right leg over your knee and keep left foot flat on ground. Hold left hand behind head, elbow bent out to side, and extend right arm by side, palm flat. Do not flatten out curve in lower back; maintain slight arch.

FINISH: Raise head, neck, and shoulders so shoulder blades clear ground, maintaining natural lower back curve. Rotate torso to right side and hold raised position without moving for 5 seconds, working up to 10. Lower and repeat. Then switch sides and repeat.

TECHNIQUE TIP: Avoid using hand to yank on head to turn torso. Instead, focus on rotating rib cage while keeping both hips anchored to ground. Keep elbow open; lead with shoulder, not arm.

MOMMY MOVE: Sing to the tune of "Little Jack Horner."

Little (baby name)
Sat in a stroller,

Watching his mommy exercise.

He sat on his bum,

And put up a thumb,

And said, "What a good boy (girl) am I!"

10. STROLLER BICYCLE

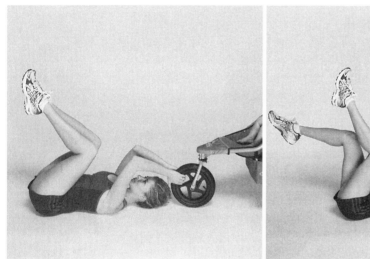

BODY BONUS: Firms core ab muscles.

START: Lie in front of stroller with top of head next to front wheel. Bring both hands over head to hold on to wheel. Then bend knees in and extend both legs straight above hips, with knees slightly bent and held close together.

FINISH: Engage abdominals and tighten whole torso to stabilize body. Slowly extend right toe away from body, abs tight. Breathe normally and bicycle legs so right toe returns to starting position as left toe extends out. Repeat.

TECHNIQUE TIP: If you feel strain in your back, your core muscles may not be strong enough to do this move yet. Focus on the

Stroller (Isometric) Crunch (page 101) to build base strength before attempting this move.

MOMMY MOVE: Sing to the tune of "Three Blind Mice."

Hi Baby,

See how much fun

We all have after we exercise,

You see mom run and jump with a big surprise.

Did you ever see such a sight in your life,

As mommy's exercise?

CHAPTER **8**

The Baby Weight Workout

There is nothing that your baby loves more than being held by you. These baby weight moves keep baby close while sneaking in a few exercises. Your sweetie will love it and you'll get a double dose of muscle-toning and baby love! In this workout you'll use a front-pack carrier with baby by your side. Cherish special moments like baby's giggle as you wobble during a lunge.

USING A BABY CARRIER

Front carriers are used from birth, or at a few weeks of age, until baby is at least six months old and can support his own head: You can then continue to use a front carrier until the recommended maximum age and weight (about thirty pounds) or you can switch to a back carrier. A properly fitted carrier is easier on your body than holding your child in your arms because it distributes weight evenly, allowing you to stand up straight instead of lop-sided while trying to balance him on your hip. Baby loves being close to you, but with a carrier you get a little bit of freedom!

This handy baby holder can also be part of a great workout. Most muscle-conditioning workouts involve the use of a dumbbell, barbell, medicine ball, or ankle weight to increase the intensity. The added weight from these devices makes muscles work harder than normal and, as a result, you get stronger and more sculpted.

Weighted vests are another resistance option. Instead of delegating the weight to your hands or ankles, the weight is strapped to your torso. You can use this exercise tool during most lower body moves and they are the recommended source of resistance for some types of cardio. (In the past, people added ankle weights or carried dumbbells to add resistance to walks or runs. Experts soon realized that the uneven weight distribution of those items increased risks of joint injury.) A weighted vest can provide the benefit of extra weight without the wear and tear to your joints.

Using a front-pack carrier adds resistance in a similar fashion. Since your child's weight is evenly distributed around your own center of gravity, it mimics a fitness weighted vest. Walking with it becomes a weight-bearing walk, allowing you to work at a higher intensity and burn more calories. The added weight may also help build more lean muscle in the lower body and may help stimulate bone density improvements to help fight osteoporosis. Even when baby is very young, those extra pounds make ordinary exercise moves more challenging and effective. And if you use the carrier early and stick with it as baby grows, you automatically get a gradual increase in weight, much like a progressive weight-training program.

WHAT YOU NEED TO KNOW
ABOUT FRONT-PACK CARRIERS

Most front-pack carriers start small babies facing the chest. After baby has sufficient head control, he can face out for a view of the world. You can tell if he's ready by his wobble factor. If his neck appears unstable and he can't hold his head up on his own, he still needs more time to grow. Follow all guidelines that come with the pack because different models may specify different age criteria. Before you buy, try on different models. Look for wide, generously padded shoulder straps and back support, a sturdy headrest that will support a sleeping baby's neck and head, and leg holes banded with soft fabric that won't irritate his skin. Choose a carrier that is easy to slip on and off by yourself without waking your baby. If you consider a sling or wrap, make sure it is completely secure.

SAFETY FIRST

- Keep all movements slow, controlled, and stable.
- Wear front-pack carrier snugly to give you and your baby the most support.
- Focusing on your exercise form may distract you from the baby. So double-check that baby is tucked in tight and straps are secure before performing any exercises.

1. FRONT PACK PLIÉ SQUAT

BODY BONUS: Firms glutes and inner thighs.

START: Tuck baby snugly into place. With hands on hips, stand in a straddle, feet wider than your shoulders. (The taller you are, or the longer your legs, the wider you should stand.) Turn toes out so they aim toward the corners.

FINISH: Inhale and bend knees, lowering hips until knees are bent around 90 degrees. Hold for three seconds. Press heels into floor as you contract glutes and inner thighs to straighten to starting position. Repeat.

TECHNIQUE TIP: You should be able to see your toes throughout the movement. If you can't, then your legs are too close. Widen stance so knees go no farther than your toes at the lowest point.

———

MOMMY MOVE: As you squat down, use your hands to do "Itsy bitsy spider . . ."

2. FRONT PACK LUNGE

BODY BONUS: Tones thighs and tightens glutes.

START: Buckle baby in and stand with feet shoulder-width apart, hands by sides. Take a wide, comfortable step three to four feet back, landing with your toe and keeping your heel lifted. Lengthen spine and stand tall, holding shoulders down and slightly back to re-sist the front pull of baby weight in front. Engage core muscles by tightening entire torso.

FINISH: Distribute body weight between front heel and back toe. Lower body by bending front knee. Stop when knee is bent around 90 degrees. Hold 3 seconds, then straighten legs to return to standing. Repeat, then switch legs.

TECHNIQUE TIP: Keep front calf vertical (perpendicular to floor) at all times. If you see knee jutting over front toe, causing calf to lean at a diagonal, step farther back.

MOMMY MOVE: While lunging, sing our version of "Looby Loo."

Here we lunge looby loo,
Here we lunge looby light.
Here we lunge looby loo,
All on a Saturday night.

3. FRONT PACK BACK EXTENSION

BODY BONUS: Strengthens lower back muscles.

START: With baby in carrier, stand with feet hip-width apart. Stand tall and lengthen spine by raising ribs. Engage your abdominals so you feel tightness throughout your entire torso. (Place hands over baby to keep head secure if needed.) Soften your knees and then, keeping your back straight with lower back in neutral if possible, slowly lean forward, leading with your chest. Stop when your back is in a diagonal line. Keep the abs braced tight as you lower.

FINISH: When torso is leaning at a 45 degree angle, squeeze glutes, hamstrings, and lower back muscles to straighten up to standing. Repeat.

TECHNIQUE TIP: Try without baby first so you don't overload your spine. Start with 2 to 4 reps and work up to recommended number. If you have back problems, then do not use baby weight. If you are starting with a brand-new baby, work up to 2 sets of 10 reps. If you are starting with an older baby (who weighs more than 15 pounds), do one set without the baby, then do another shorter set with baby of just 6 to 8 reps. If you feel any strain on your back, omit this exercise from your routine.

MOMMY MOVE: This is a fun one for "Jack-in-the-Box": "Jack-in-the-box sits so still. Won't you come out? Yes, I will." Carefully hold your bent position for the first verse and come up like the Jack-in-the-box for the last verse.

4. SUPERMANS

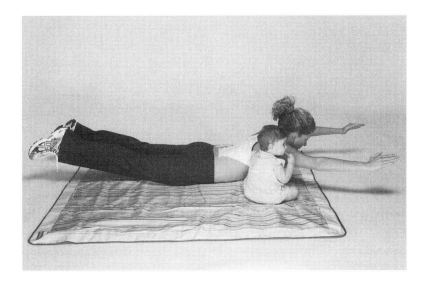

BODY BONUS: Strengthens back muscles.

START: Lie face-down on stomach with legs straight. Raise arms above head and drop forehead to floor.

FINISH: Tighten glutes and simultaneously raise thighs and upper arms an inch or two off floor. Hold, then lower and repeat.

TECHNIQUE TIP: If you feel strain in your lower back, modify move by raising only one leg or arm at a time.

MOMMY MOVE: Slowly sing the ABCs as you rise in Superman position. As you get stronger, see how far you can get through the song while holding yourself up.

5. FRONT-PACK SCAPULAR RETRACTION

BODY BONUS: Fight breastfeeding- or baby-carrying-induced shoulder slump by strengthening your upper back. Do this exercise every time you wear your front-pack carrier in regular, everyday mommy life!

START: With baby on board, stand with feet shoulder-width apart, arms by your sides. Stand tall and lift out of your lower back.

FINISH: Imagine that your shoulder blades are plates covering each side of your upper back. Exhale as you contract the upper back muscles to slide the plates closer toward each other, allowing your arms to move back slightly as you do. Hold for 3 seconds, then inhale as you release, separating shoulder blades while still maintaining perfect, erect posture. Repeat.

TECHNIQUE TIP: Be careful not to wear your shoulders as earrings! Keep shoulders low and neck long throughout move.

MOMMY MOVE: Because hands are free with the front-pack carrier, you can do a finger play. Try "Round and Round the Garden."

Round and round the garden, Round and round the garden,
Goes the Teddy Bear, One Step, Two Steps,
Tickle Him Under . . . There! (walk fingers up chest and tickle baby)

6. BABY PLANK

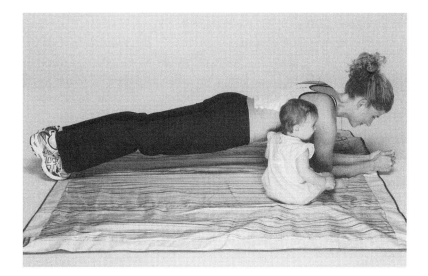

BODY BONUS: Develops endurance in core muscles that help support the lower back.

START: Lie on your stomach with legs extended and prop your-self up on your forearms. Lower shoulders.

FINISH: Pull in abs away from floor to engage muscles in entire torso, raise hips off floor. Raise one knee at a time off floor until you are in a raised plank position, body forming a straight line from head to toe. Make sure hips neither sag to floor, nor pike and press up. Breathe normally. Hold, then rest and repeat.

TECHNIQUE TIP: If lower back hurts, build up to exercise by first doing it resting on knees with just the hips and torso raised. Hold 5 to 10 seconds and work up to 30 seconds in both variations.

MOMMY MOVE: This is a tough move so you might want to pass on singing. Instead, count SLOWLY in Spanish. If you do it often enough, your child will start picking it up. As you get stronger, you'll have to learn new numbers!

7. BABY PUSH-UP

BODY BONUS: Builds up chest strength in your pectoral muscles.

START: Lie on back with knees bent and feet flat on the ground. Sit baby on top of your ribs so you are tummy to tummy with his or her legs straddling your waist. Maintain a slight arch in your lower back by tightening your abs without pressing your spine flat to floor.

FINISH: Hold baby firmly on either side of his body. As you exhale, push him straight above you until your arms are straight. Slowly lower and repeat.

TECHNIQUE TIP: To avoid straining shoulders, hold baby over your ribs, rather than higher up by your face.

MOMMY MOVE: When you push baby up sing our version of "One little, two little Indians":

One little, two little, three little push-ups,
Four little, five little, six little push-ups,
Seven little, eight little, nine little push-ups,
Ten little push-ups in a row.

8. BABY HIP BRIDGE

BODY BONUS: Firms your glutes while baby gets a ride!

START: Lie on your back with knees bent, feet flat. Hold baby securely facing you on top of your abdomen.

FINISH: Squeeze your glutes and raise hips about 3 inches off the ground. Hold, then slowly lower and repeat.

TECHNIQUE TIP: If your back feels strain, tilt pelvis slightly and focus on squeezing glutes rather than lifting your torso high.

———

MOMMY MOVE: Sing "London Bridge Is Falling Down" as you pulse your hips at top. Drop hips down every time you sing the word "down."

9. BABY CURL-UPS

BODY BONUS: Firms up your midsection.

START: Lie on back with knees bent and feet flat on ground. Sit baby on top of your abs with his or her legs straddling your waist. Try not to completely flatten out curve in lower back. Instead, maintain slight arch by tightening your abs without distorting spine.

FINISH: Raise head, neck, and shoulders so shoulder blades just clear the ground, all the while maintaining natural curve in lower back. Reach arms out to either side of baby to make a fence around him. Rather than move body forward, hold raised position without moving for 15 seconds, working up to 30 seconds. Lower and repeat.

TECHNIQUE TIP: If your neck fatigues, shorten your holds. If your lower back feels strained, place a small rolled-up towel under the hollow of your lower back for extra spinal support.

MOMMY MOVE: As you hold the position, do our version of "One Potato, Two Potato."

One curl-up, two curl-up, three curl-up, four,
Five curl-up, six curl-up, seven curl-up more.

10. BABY REVERSE CURL

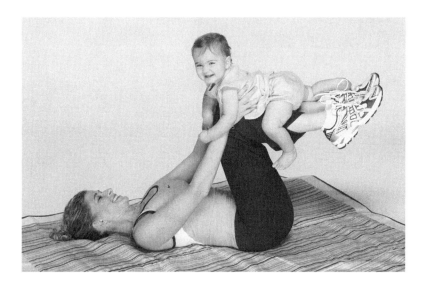

BODY BONUS: Firms up your abs.

START: Lie on your back and hold baby on your chest. Then bend knees and bring both legs into chest. Rest baby on your shins.

FINISH: As you exhale, contract abs so that hips tilt slightly forward, and lower back rises slightly off the ground. Hold, then slowly lower and repeat.

TECHNIQUE TIP: To avoid straining back, make sure not to let feet drop too close to floor; keep all weight above abs and torso.

MOMMY MOVE: Baby will be happy as she moves through the air in this movement. Need a song? How about an airplane rhyme?

Oh, look, see our airplanes,
Away up in the sky,
Watch us gliding through the air,
This is how we fly.

CHAPTER 9

The Mom-Has-Just-a-Minute Workout

Some days, you'll only have time to pull out your tubing and dash through a few moves. This is a workout you can do anywhere, anytime. Place baby near you so that you can watch her as you execute the moves (and so that he or she can watch mommy do funny things with rubber tubes!). Or if she needs to be held or if you are incorporating the exercises while out on a walk, keep her in her stroller. Follow the tubing safety guidelines on page 75.

TUBING TECHNIQUES AT A GLANCE

- Hold handles with a loose grip. Don't squeeze.
- Keep wrists in neutral during exercises.
- Tighten slack by shortening tube or pulling it further to keep sufficient resistance.
- Like any other exercise, breathe! The general rule is to exhale on exertion.

1. WALL SQUAT

BODY BONUS: Builds endurance in your thighs.

START: Find a wall and position baby to face wall. Stand with your back against wall, facing baby. Keeping your back on the wall, step out away from wall until your feet are 2 to 3 feet in front of you.

FINISH: Slide your back down wall until hips are knee level. Tighten abs and carry body weight in your heels. Hold for a song, then slide up and repeat.

TECHNIQUE TIP: If knees feel strained, walk feet farther away from body and/or lower to a higher point above knee level.

MOMMY MOVE: This is a favorite song stop. Play pattycake or sing "B-I-N-G-O." In Stroller Strides we modify: "If you're happy and you know it, shout Stroller Strides!"

2. STEP-UPS

BODY BONUS: Firms glutes and thighs, and sneaks in a cardio interval, too.

START: If indoors, use bottom step on your staircase or porch (or pull out an aerobics step if you have one). Outdoors, find a sturdy bench or step. Then place your right foot flat on top. Make sure heel is not hanging over edge. Keep hands by sides.

FINISH: Press body weight into your right foot and shift yourself up to the top of the step, bringing your left foot to touch the step. Hold, then lower and repeat on the same leg. Switch sides and repeat.

TECHNIQUE TIP: Start with a low step, then work your way up to higher steps or benches.

ADVANCED OPTION: Did you take step aerobics classes before baby? Create your own step workout by doing knee-ups, hip extensions, repeaters, and other moves that you remember.

MOMMY MOVE: Step-ups get your heart pumping so it might be hard to sing. Instead, practice counting out loud. Do sets of 10 on each leg and before you know it, baby will learn the count even if she can't repeat it yet.

3. TUBING BICEPS CURL

BODY BONUS: Strengthens biceps (and will make carrying baby-carrying easier).

START: Hold tube handles by your sides, with arms hanging straight. Place middle of tube under your feet, standing with feet about hip-width apart, knees bent slightly, and abdomen tight. If there is any slack on either side of tube, or if it is so short that you feel hunched forward, adjust your feet closer or wider so tube is taut, but has room to stretch.

FINISH: With palms facing up, exhale and slowly bring hands from sides up toward your shoulders, keeping elbows fixed at side. Pause at top of position and contract biceps, then inhale and slowly lower hands back to starting position. Repeat.

TECHNIQUE TIP: If your elbows feel strained, do one arm at a time or lengthen the tube.

MOMMY MOVE: This song will teach baby (and maybe you) how to count in Spanish . . .

Uno, dos, y tres,
Cuatro, cinco, y seis.
Siete, ocho, y nueve,
Cuento hasta diez.

One, two, and three,
Four, five, and six.
Seven, eight, and nine,
I count to ten.

4. TUBING SHOULDER PRESS

BODY BONUS: Strengthens shoulders and upper back.

START: Hold on to both ends of tube, then step into its middle with right foot. Reach left leg back about 3 feet behind and balance on back toe; heel stays lifted. Bend front knee slightly, then bend elbows, bringing hands up as if doing a biceps curl, then keep raising arms until your elbows are opened by sides at shoulder level. Your hands should be held directly over each elbow, so your arms are bent at 90 degrees. Your palms should face forward.

FINISH: As you exhale, press both hands overhead until your arms are straight. If you feel any neck or upper back tension, or your ability to move smoothly is limited, lower your hips to provide more tube length. Or, switch to a lighter-resistance tube. Inhale and lower to starting position. Repeat.

TECHNIQUE TIP: If you have any shoulder discomfort, rotate palms inward so that they face each other, rather than to front.

ADVANCED OPTION: Step on tube with both feet to increase the intensity.

MOMMY MOVE: Recite one letter of the alphabet ("A is for apple") as you do each rep.

5. TUBING ROW

BODY BONUS: Strengthens upper back, biceps, and the back of shoulders to ward off mommy hunch.

START: Hold handles in each hand as you grasp a short portion of middle of tube so it can be stretched taut when you straighten arms directly in front of chest. (Loop extra slack on sides over your hands.) Stand with feet apart, legs in slight split stance, left in front of right. Hold out palms at shoulder level, facing down.

FINISH: Engage abs to keep torso steady as you tighten upper back muscles and exhale as you pull your hands apart to stretch tube as you pull elbows backward, stopping just past rib cage. Feel shoulder blades slide toward each other. Pause, then inhale and slowly extend arms in front back to starting position. Repeat.

TECHNIQUE TIP: Make sure you feel a sufficient pull during the lifting and lowering phase. Get rid of slack by wrapping the end of the tube a couple more times around your hand.

OPTIONS: If you are out on a stroller walk, do this move by bringing tube through a link on the fence. The tube is anchored on the fence instead of being held in front of you. If you want to increase intensity, step farther away from the fence. (See Stroller Workout on page 91.)

MOMMY MOVE: This one is a natural for "Row, Row, Row Your Boat."

6. TUBING SHOULDER RAISE

BODY BONUS: Develops firm, sculpted shoulders by targeting your medial and front deltoids.

START (not shown): Stand on the middle of your tube with your feet shoulder-width apart and your knees bent slightly. Hold the handles of the tube in each hand. Palms face down, held just in front of thighs, arms slightly bent. Engage all abdominal muscles by tightening entire torso.

MIDDLE MOVE: Exhale as you slowly raise one arm in front, keeping it straight with palm facing down. Lift as high as shoulder level if you can keep arms slightly bent. Find the range of motion in which you can complete move while maintaining good posture. Pause at top and inhale as you slowly return to start. Repeat on other arm. Lower and face both palms inward.

SECOND MOVE: From starting position, exhale as you slowly raise arms sideways. Lift as high as shoulder level if you can keep arms in and slightly bent. (Most moms find that they need to stop raising their arms at a lower level to maintain proper form.) Pause at top and then inhale as you slowly return to start position. Repeat.

TECHNIQUE TIP: Make sure to keep head and neck relaxed throughout movement and avoid scrunching shoulders by your ears. If the exercise feels too difficult, try raising one arm at a time, alternating sides. If you feel shoulder discomfort, rotate palms into a shoulder-neutral position: palms facing each other.

MOMMY MOVE: Change arm motion to go along with "Wheels on the Bus." Here's a sample:

The wheels on the bus go round and round
(arms do little circles in the raised position)
The wipers on the bus go swish swish swish
(arms do a side raise)
The people on the bus go up and down
(arms do a forward lift right in front of body)
The horn on the bus goes beep beep beep
(do a small but controlled pulse at your highest point of either exercise)

7. TUBING LAT PULL-DOWN

BODY BONUS: Strengthens your upper and middle back muscles.

START: Hold the handles in each hand as you grasp a portion of the tube so that it can be stretched taut when you straighten your arms overhead. (Loop any extra slack on the sides over your hands.) Stand with your feet as wide as you comfortably can, feet and knees facing out, and extend the arms straight up, palms facing front.

FINISH: As you exhale, stretch the tube wider and pull it down in front of your chest by lowering your elbows out to the sides, stopping when your elbows are about rib cage level and your hands open wide to the side at shoulder level. Repeat.

TECHNIQUE TIP: Keep your shoulders low when your arms are extended overhead, then focus on sliding your shoulder blades down and together to engage your back muscles.

INTENSITY OPTIONS:

1. To make it easier, do one arm at a time, so one arm remains at top while the other pulls down.

2. Combine the Lat Pull-down with a Front Pack Plié Squat (see page 110). By combining two exercises, you'll get twice the workout in half the time.

MOMMY MOVE: At this station, teach your little one about the sounds animals make. Each time you do a rep, name an animal and make his sound. For instance, "A dog goes woof" for repetition one, "A cat goes meow" for repetition two, and so on.

8. SHOULDER ROTATION

BODY BONUS: Strengthens the rotator cuff muscles to keep the upper back strong and the joints aligned. This is great for many mommies who experience sharp shoulder pain from holding baby constantly and from having their shoulder blades pulled.

START: Hold handles in each hand as you grasp a short portion in middle of tube so it can be stretched taut when you hold your elbows by your sides and extend your forearms directly out in front of waist. (Loop extra slack on sides over hands.) Stand with legs shoulder-width apart and rotate palms up.

FINISH: Keep elbows tucked close to sides as you contract muscles in upper back to rotate forearms outward. Move hands out to sides and stop when forearms form a V. Feel shoulder blades flatten closer to ribs in back. Slowly slide forearms toward each other, feeling shoulder blades separate as you return to start. Repeat.

TECHNIQUE TIP: Think of your elbows like hinges on a door. The hinges stay attached to the frame as the door opens and shuts just as your elbows stay attached to your sides as the arms open and shut.

———

MOMMY MOVE: Change "Old MacDonald" so it incorporates baby's name.

Little (baby's name) has a farm

E-I-E-I-O

And on that farm she has some (name an animal)

E-I-E-I-O

With a (animal sound) here and a (animal sound) there

Here a (animal sound) and there a (animal sound)

Everywhere a (animal sound), (animal sound)

Little (baby's name) has a farm

E-I-E-I-O

9A. STANDING TRICEPS EXTENSION

BODY BONUS: Strengthens triceps.

START: Place one end of exercise tube securely under right foot and stand with feet hip-width apart and knees slightly bent. Grasp right handle with right hand. Bring hand behind head so elbow is bent at a 90 degree angle and pointing toward the ceiling. Do not bend arm more than 90 degrees. Palm faces in.

FINISH: With back straight and abdominals tight, exhale as you slowly extend arm, straightening your elbow and moving hand above head so arm is vertical and pointing up. Pause, and inhale as you slowly return to start. Repeat, then switch sides.

TECHNIQUE TIP: Use your free hand to stabilize upper arm. If shoulder position feels uncomfortable, do the Triceps Kickback instead on pages 142–143.

———

MOMMY MOVE: Sing a count-down song. As you get stronger, you'll get closer to finishing the song . . .

There were ten in a bed and the little one said,
"Roll over, roll over."
So they all rolled over and one fell out.
There were nine in the bed and the little one said,
"Roll over, roll over."
So they all rolled over and one fell out . . .
There was one in the bed and the little one said,
"Good night!"

9B. TRICEPS KICKBACK (option to 9A)

BODY BONUS: Firms back of upper arms.

START: Place end of exercise tube under your left foot and stand with legs in split stance, right leg behind left. Grasp left handle with left hand. Bend knees slightly and engage abs as you lean slightly over front thigh with a straight back. Rest right hand on left thigh to support weight of upper body. With palm facing in, pull left hand back, hugging left elbow close to rib cage.

FINISH: Keeping upper arm anchored in place, exhale and extend arm back by pulling on tube and straightening elbow. Pause at top, then slowly bend elbow to return to start. Repeat, then switch sides. (Adjust length of tube by moving foot closer or farther from end. Tube should be taut throughout.)

TECHNIQUE TIP: Avoid flexing, or bending, wrist. Instead, keep it rigid so that it is straight in line with forearms.

MOMMY MOVE: Modify "This Little Piggy Went to Market."

This little baby went out to play,
This little baby stayed home,
This little baby got big and strong,
This little baby had no fun,
This little baby played and played and ran all the way home.

10. CHEST PRESS

BODY BONUS: Firms up pectoral muscles.

START: Wrap tube around your back and hold a handle in each hand in front of body, elbows raised sideways to shoulder level, hands held at shoulder level directly in front of elbows. Stand in a split-leg stance, left leg slightly in front of right, both toes aiming forward.

FINISH: Stand tall and engage abs as you exhale and push both hands directly in front of chest to straighten arms. Pause, then move elbows out to sides to starting position and repeat.

TECHNIQUE TIP: Keep shoulders down throughout move.

OPTIONS: If you are out on a stroller walk, you can loop your tube through a link on a fence. Step away from the fence to create more intensity.

MOMMY MOVE: Sing our version of "She'll Be Coming Around
the Mountain."

I'll be coming to tickle you,
Yes I will.
I'll be coming to tickle you,
Yes I will.
I'll be coming to tickle
Just as soon as I finish this exercise,
Yes I'll be coming to tickle you yes I will.

CHAPTER **10**

The Stretching Workout

After all your challenging workouts, you deserve a little pampering with these relaxing stretches. If baby isn't already asleep, you can sing soft lullabies as you stretch. You can do these stretches on their own, or after any cardio session or any of the three workouts.

Staying flexible is the key to combating the tightness you feel from a stressed or busy lifestyle, or from the constant lugging of heavy baby accessories. All exercise increases the range of motion around a joint, so you will become more flexible simply by doing regular workouts. But you can maximize your flexibility by doing specific stretches that target specific muscles.

To stretch, all you need to do is lengthen a muscle to release tension. Always stretch to a range that feels pleasant, not painful. If you push a stretch too deep, then you trigger a protective response by the muscle that causes it to contract in order to prevent it from over-stretching. Obviously, this is counterproductive to what you are trying to achieve. So, even if you think you are very inflexible, don't push past your current limits. Your muscles will let you know how far you can take a stretch on any given day. (You may be tighter in the mornings or on cold days, and looser on warm days or in the afternoon, for example.)

Take it easy: Avoid aiming for hyper-flexibility, since joints need to be able to retain some stiffness around them to stay rigid under stress. For example, if you are jogging with overly flexible hip and knee joints, it may be difficult for your limbs to stay aligned and symmetrical while you run. Over time, that can cause stress imbalances that can lead to injuries. Or, if you were to trip on the pavement, a joint may be more likely to twist in an unnatural way, and perhaps tear, rather than stay stable and aligned. Some extreme stretching moves that can be found in yoga, for example, can stretch more than the muscle around a joint. They can also overstretch your ligaments around the joint, causing the joint to become chronically unstable. One reason joints tend to be weaker after you've had an injury—a sprained ankle or twisted knee, for example—is because the ligaments have been overstretched. Ligaments have very little elasticity, so once they are looser, they are unlikely to spring back to their healthy length.

As a new mom, you may have enjoyed greater flexibility during pregnancy. This is due to the hormone relaxin, which helps your body expand as baby grows. After birth, these effects can last for up to twelve weeks, or longer if you are breastfeeding. That means that you should be cautious about overstretching at first. Having noted that caution, there is little research that shows you could be injured due to this increased flexibility. Certain areas of your body will be tighter or more stretched from your new duties as a mom. Bending over and picking up baby, or hunching over to breastfeed can make your upper back muscles loose and your chest muscles tight. So stretch what's tight, but don't overstretch what's already loose, like your upper back.

When you stretch, just relax. Use your breathing to help loosen the muscles. Inhale and exhale deeply (through your nostrils preferably and filling up down to the base of your lungs). Lengthen each exhalation so it comes out very slowly. Pause before you breathe in and out.

Singing soothing melodies to your baby may also help relax you. If you're listening to gentle music, let your body move and flow with the sound. When you exhale, you may notice a release in muscle tension. Usually you will feel a tight muscle become more flexible after holding a static stretch from ten to thirty seconds. Try not to bounce or force it. Just luxuriate in the process.

Mommy Moves: For this section, we did not include mommy songs or activities so you can take a time out to stretch and get a moment of quiet. Pull out a toy or activity to entertain baby. If she's been in the stroller for the workout, she may be happy to get out and play on her blanket next to you while you stretch. Learn how to find a moment of peace even when there is chaos around you!

For all stretches listed, with the exception of the Side Reach, be sure to put on the stroller brake.

1. STROLLER SIDE REACH

BODY BONUS: Stretches your tight torso.

START: Take brake off stroller so that it glides as you move. Place right hand on handlebar for balance and open legs to a wide straddle. Raise left arm out to left side.

FINISH: Lift ribs away from pelvis to lengthen lower back and exhale as you reach left arm up and over your head. Hold and focus on elongating your spine. As you reach, push stroller away from you. Lower arm and tilt your torso back to a vertical position, bringing stroller back in. Switch sides and repeat.

TECHNIQUE TIP: Rather than bending as much as possible, lift your body as high as possible.

2. GLUTE STRETCH

BODY BONUS: Loosens up tight glutes.

MOVEMENT: Stand next to stroller and hold on to handlebar with right hand. Lift left knee up to left hip and hold on to it with left hand. Hold thigh close to body to feel stretch in glutes. Switch sides and repeat.

TECHNIQUE TIP: Try not to press too hard on top of knee. If you feel any discomfort, place hand between back thigh and back of knee.

ADVANCED OPTION: Turn this move into an advanced stretch by letting go of the stroller and doing it as a balancing pose. Raise right arm to sky.

3. STROLLER QUAD STRETCH

BODY BONUS: Stretches the front of your upper thighs and hip flexors.

MOVEMENT: Stand next to stroller and hold on to handlebar with right hand. Lift left knee up to front of left hip and gently hold on to left foot with left hand. Then, *without twisting your knee*, move foot down, under hip and to back so that hand is not holding on to foot, with bent knee pointing down and foot by your rear. Squeeze glutes to feel stretch in your quadriceps and hip flexors. Switch sides and repeat.

TECHNIQUE TIP: To increase stretch, do not pull harder on foot;

instead, press left hip slightly forward. If your bent knee feels strained, loosen grip on foot and open knee to a wider bent angle.

ADVANCED OPTION: Turn this move into an advanced stretch by letting go of the stroller and doing it as a balancing pose. Raise arm to sky.

4. STROLLER HIP AND BUTT STRETCH

BODY BONUS: Loosens hips and helps sciatic tightness.

MOVEMENT: Stand in front of stroller and hold on to handlebar with both hands. Lift left foot up and cross your left calf over top of right thigh. Sit back, holding weight in heel to feel stretch in piriformis muscle in your rear. Hold, then switch sides.

TECHNIQUE TIP: If top knee feels uncomfortable, try not to twist it by dropping knee too low to get a deep stretch. Sit back instead of down, pulling hips back toward horizon.

5. STROLLER HAMSTRING STRETCH

BODY BONUS: Stretches back of thighs.

MOVEMENT: Stand in front of stroller and hold on to handlebar with right hand. Lift left leg and place left heel on wheel and rest left hand on top of your thigh. Lean torso forward at a diagonal and press hips back to feel stretch in back of thigh. Hold, then switch sides.

TECHNIQUE TIP: Flex toe to sneak in a calf stretch.

6. STROLLER CALF STRETCH

BODY BONUS: Loosens tight calves.

MOVEMENT: Stand in front of stroller and hold on to handlebar with right hand. Lift left toe and place it against left wheel, heel on ground. Lean body forward into the stretch. Hold, then switch sides.

TECHNIQUE TIP: Stretch just enough to feel a pull in calf muscle in back of lower leg, but not so deep that you strain your Achilles tendon in back of the heel.

7. SHOULDER STRETCH

BODY BONUS: Loosens shoulders.

MOVEMENT: Stand next to stroller and cross left arm over your chest. Hold elbow with right hand and pull upper arm farther across to feel a stretch in back of left shoulder. Hold, then switch sides.

TECHNIQUE TIP: Don't overdo this stretch, especially if you feel like you're developing shoulder slump from holding baby.

8. TRICEPS STRETCH

BODY BONUS: Stretches back of upper arms.

MOVEMENT: Stand by stroller and extend right arm straight above you, pointing to ceiling. Bend right elbow, dropping right hand behind head. Imagine reaching down your spine. Hold on to right elbow with left hand and pull upper arm slightly backward so you feel a stretch in back. Hold, then switch sides.

TECHNIQUE TIP: If you feel any discomfort in your shoulder, drop elbow slightly to front.

9. SPINAL TWIST

BODY BONUS: Increases range of motion and releases tension in your torso.

MOVEMENT: Sit next to stroller and extend both legs straight in front of you. Bend right knee and cross leg over bottom leg, placing right foot on outside of left knee. Sit tall and try to lengthen your spine as you reach left arm over right thigh, pressing left elbow against outside of right thigh to shift bent leg toward left side as you simultaneously rotate torso to right.

TECHNIQUE TIP: Hold both shoulders down as you turn torso.

10. CHEST STRETCH

BODY BONUS: Loosens tight chest muscles. Chest stretches are important to the posture of a new mom. So make time to fit these in daily.

MOVEMENT: Stand by stroller and open arms out to side in a T position with palms facing up and thumbs to the back. Push thumbs an inch or two backward until you feel a pleasant stretch in chest and upper inner arm.

TECHNIQUE TIP: Keep shoulders low, not hunched.

Some Other Chest Stretches:

1. Hold a towel taut overhead with an end in each hand. Open arms back until you feel a nice stretch.

2. Stand facing a corner, with both hands at shoulder height on each adjoining wall. Lean body into the corner, bending elbows out to the sides until you feel the stretch.

CHAPTER **11**

What You Eat

You may feel like you have less time than ever to worry about what you eat. Eating well is not only important for breastfeeding, but for giving you energy and getting you back into shape. This chapter covers nutrition basics and gives ideas on how to improve how you and your family eat.

One thing that virtually all new moms have in common is the desire to lose weight. But when you're consumed with motherhood, you may feel too busy to eat right or follow a diet. Or you may not know where to begin if you are restricted from dieting because you are breastfeeding.

What will help you lose your baby weight is making smart eating choices and being consistent about sticking to them. The *Lean Mommy* plan is not a diet. It's about making healthier improvements to the way you eat now. At this special point in your life, you really don't have time to get nitpicky about every bite that goes into your mouth. A drastic overhaul of what you eat is not realistic. This plan assumes that you know the basics—that a balanced diet of whole foods (plenty of fresh fruits and vegetables, nuts, beans, and whole grains, and healthy selections of fish, poultry, meat, and some dairy) is the way to go. And if you do eat something that isn't the most nutritious choice, like a cheese Danish, then you know to limit portions.

Scan the sections in the next chapter to find tips that jump out at you and that you can easily adopt. Pick a few changes that you feel you can realistically make. If all you did is modify a meal that you eat every day so that you save 100 calories, you could lose ten pounds in a year from that tiny tweak alone. Make a few more simple changes and lose more. And when you couple the smart food choices with exercise, in a year you could lose even more baby weight, depending upon how active you are.

BREASTFEEDING DOS AND DON'TS

If you haven't yet decided whether to nurse, consider the amazing benefits: Breast milk is far more nutritious than formula and has been shown to help boost a baby's immune system. And your health benefits, too. Women who breastfeed have a lower risk of contracting some diseases, including ovarian and uterine cancers, type 2 diabetes, and osteoporosis. Plus, you're less likely to become obese later.

Women who breastfeed shouldn't diet because cutting calories can affect the nutrient quality and quantity of milk. Some women are so eager to drop weight that they opt not to breastfeed for this very reason. If you are unable to breastfeed, formula is a good substitute. But choosing not to do it for vanity alone is putting yourself before your baby.

Besides, nursing doesn't mean that you'll be unable to lose weight. In fact, studies have shown that breastfeeders take off pregnancy weight more easily and are more likely to keep it off. It takes about 20 calories to create an ounce of milk. The average that most nursing moms create is a quart a day. That can add up to 200 to 500 calories burned per day. Some moms say that they can't get off the last 5 pounds when nursing. This might be because the body needs that weight to produce the quality and quantity needed of breast milk. I can tell you from personal experience that I have never been as lean as when I was nursing. I was eating well but still dropping pounds.

Breastfeeding can be tough to master. My entire first six weeks of motherhood were focused on both me and my baby learning how to nurse with the help of a lactation consultant. If you are able, breastfeed for at least six months, if not the full first year of your baby's life.

Make sure to modify *daily* habits. If you only eat donuts once a month and decide to substitute whole grain toast with jam instead, that's great, but the switch won't have as much of an impact as if you dropped from three teaspoons of sugar to one in the coffee drink that you have every single day, or if you were to cut out the croutons in a salad eaten with every dinner.

GOLDEN RULES OF GOOD NUTRITION

GO FOR COLOR

One easy way to take in the variety of nutrients that you and your family need is to make every meal as colorful as possible. Nutrients in plants known as phytochemicals are often found in the pigment that gives a food its hue. So create a plate that has plenty of green, red, orange, and yellow foods. Healthful beans and grains and meats, poultry, and fish will add neutral shades of white, beige, brown, and pink.

GET A HANDLE ON PORTION SIZES

Every food has calories. So, in theory, if you eat too much of anything, you can gain weight. (But I'm still looking for the person who got fat eating too many strawberries and oranges.) The truth is, fresh foods usually have lots of fiber and so it's hard to eat too much of them. Processed foods like pasta, animal products like cheese and oils, on the other hand, are calorically dense, which makes it easy to overload on them. Learn what a sensible portion really is. (And no, it's not the two-foot-wide plate you're given at some family restaurants!) Read labels and notice if the food says three servings for the whole can or box you were about to eat.

KNOW YOUR GOOD CARBS FROM YOUR BAD CARBS

Plant ingredients like wheat grains that have been processed into manufactured foods like pasta or bread are known as bad carbs. High-sugar foods are, too. These foods are broken down quickly and

SUPERFOODS FOR NEW MOMS

DAIRY—Look for organic, no-hormone products. When possible, choose white cheese over yellow. Choose low-fat dairy options for yourself (but not your toddlers).			
Cottage cheese	Ricotta cheese	Milk	
Goat cheese	Whole milk cheese	Muenster cheese	
Yogurt	Kefir	Feta cheese	
LEAN MEAT, FISH, POULTRY, AND EGGS—If possible, use hormone-free, antibiotic-free, range-fed.			
Tuna	Halibut	Tilapia	
Salmon	Shark	Lean beef	
White meat chicken	White meat pork	White meat turkey	
Eggs			
FATS AND OILS—Use sparingly. These fats are safe to use while cooking.			
Butter	Extra virgin olive oil	Almond oil	
Avocado oil	Canola oil	Grapeseed oil	
FRUITS—Best if fresh or frozen and organic, preferably from local farms.			
Apples	Dates	Mangos	Pineapples
Apricots	Figs	Melons	Plums
Avocados	Grapefruit	Nectarines	Pomegranates
Bananas	Grapes	Oranges	Prunes
Blackberries	Guavas	Papayas	Raisins
Blueberries	Kiwis	Peaches	Strawberries

Boysenberries	Lemons	Pears	Tangerines
Cherries	Limes	Persimmons	Watermelon

VEGETABLES—Best if fresh or frozen and organic, preferably from local farms.

Bell peppers	Collard greens	Jicama	Radishes
Broccoli	Cucumber	Kale	Snow peas
Brussels sprouts	Eggplant	Lettuce	Spinach
Cabbage	Fennel	Mushrooms	Squash
Carrots	Garlic	Onions	Sweet potatoes
Cauliflower	Green beans	Parsley	Tomatoes
Celery	Hearts of palm	Peppers	

NUTS AND SEEDS—Good source of protein, carbohydrates, and fat.

Pecans	Cashews	Pine nuts	Almonds
Macadamia nuts	Walnuts	Sunflower seeds	Pumpkin seeds
Peanut butter	Other nut and seed butters		

GRAINS AND LEGUMES—Good source of protein, carbohydrates, fiber, and vitamins.

Dried beans	Barley	Lentils	
Buckwheat	Brown rice	Couscous	
Whole grains	Spelt	Whole grain breakfast cereals	
Wild rice	Whole grain pasta	Quinoa	

(continued on next page)

SNACK			
Whole grain pretzels	Rye crispbread		
Whole grain rice cakes	Rye wafers (Wasa)		
Baked corn tortilla chips	Wheat melba toast		

tend to be absorbed into the body very quickly, too. This is not a problem unless you are overweight and inactive and are glucose intolerant. Then too much insulin may be released to help carry the glucose into the cells of your body that use it for energy. Over time, this overload can lead to diabetes. Active people do not need to worry about this. In fact, endurance exercisers running races or going on long bike rides need to take in some bad carbs, such as sports drinks, to fuel them when their body starts to fatigue.

On the other hand, white processed carbs are not the healthiest choice because the fiber and many nutrients are stripped out. So you will always make a better choice when you choose brown rice over white rice or whole grain bread over white. And you'd make an even better choice if you choose the whole grains themselves over a food product that contains them: You can buy kernels of rye, wheat, barley, quinoa, and other grains in bins at whole food stores and boil them like rice, add seasoning, and serve with any other food.

PICK PROTEIN CAREFULLY

Protein is the term for the different amino acids. Amino acids, or protein, are found in all foods in varying amounts. So not only do meat, fish, peanuts, beans, and milk contain protein, so do broccoli, rice, and asparagus! There are eleven amino acids that cannot be made within our bodies. So they must come from food. If you eat a variety of healthy foods, you'll have no trouble obtaining all the needed amino acids. That's why a vegetarian who eats only plant foods will have no problem getting enough protein if they eat a healthy range of foods. Animal foods—meat, fish, poultry, eggs, and dairy—contain all eleven of these amino acids within one food. They are called "complete" for that reason. But research shows that we should take in a higher proportion of protein from plant foods than from animal foods. So when you think protein, don't just think meat, think vegetables, nuts, beans, and grains, too. When eating animal protein sources, go for organic, grass-fed, low-fat, and/or lean when you can.

CHOOSE GOOD FATS

Not only are fats yummy, some are beneficial to your health. Animal fats in meats, poultry, and dairy products are mostly saturated fats since they have a chemical structure that makes them solid. That's why you can cut off a piece of fat from a steak or slice through butter or cheese. Less than 10 percent of the fat you eat should be saturated. Unsaturated fats are found in all foods, but are the predominant fat in plant foods. They have been shown to help reduce, not raise, your levels of bad cholesterol (your LDLs) and raise levels of your good cholesterol (HDLs). So that's why, even though foods like olives, avocados, and nuts can have a high percentage of fat, they're still great for you. Unsaturated fats tend to be liquid (sunflower, walnut, olive, and corn oils). Trans fats are good fats gone bad. Food manufacturers take a healthy oil, like soybean oil, and modify it in a process called hydrogenization so that it becomes solid, and more like saturated fat. Think Crisco or margarine. It's cheap and has a longer shelf life. So that's why most fast food restaurants and big companies that make packaged foods use loads of the stuff. The problem is, no known amount of trans fat is considered safe. It not only raises your LDLs, it lowers your HDLs, and increases your risk of heart disease. The best way to avoid it is to stop eating processed, packaged foods. If you eat home-cooked or fresh-prepared, you'll mostly avoid it. (Just don't cook with Crisco or margarine.) If you do eat packaged foods, look for 0 grams of trans fat on the label.

NO-NO FOODS FOR NEW MOMS AND KIDS

While I hate to ban foods, and would never do so directly to my children, there are a few items that you should avoid:

SODAS: Avoid getting hooked on the addictive taste of soft drinks (even diet). There is nothing beneficial about them. Studies have shown that kids who drink more sodas tend to drink less milk, and therefore reduce the calcium intake that is necessary for growing bones.

DONUTS, PASTRIES: Both store-bought and packaged donuts are high in sugar and often loaded with trans fats. They don't offer much in the way of nutrients except for extra calories. When you or your kids fill up on foods that lack vitamins and minerals, there is less room for the foods that do provide necessary nutrients.

FRIED, CRUNCHY THINGIES: Salty snacks and potato chips can be addictive. But these foods offer very little in the way of nutrients.

KID'S MEALS: Do they really need a cheap toy if it also includes a healthy wallop of fat, sugar, and calories? Kid's menus are loaded with fried, fatty items like chicken nuggets, burgers, fries, and macaroni and cheese. Instead, share your dish, or order a half-portion of something better from the adult menu. Buy or bring your own plastic toy if that reward is so important.

FAKE FRUIT SNACKS: Prepackaged fruit snacks such as Fruit Roll-Ups are filled with sugar, sugar, more sugar, and about a dozen chemicals I can't pronounce. Dried fruit is okay because it has fiber and antioxidants.

FOODS WITH HIGH-FRUCTOSE CORN SYRUP: This highly processed, fake sweetener is cheap, which is why you'll find it in candy, fruit, and chocolate drinks and even ketchup. It has been linked to the obesity epidemic and rising rates of diabetes. So read labels and avoid it when you can.

NITRATE-CONTAINING HOT DOGS AND SANDWICH MEATS: Nitrates are preservatives used in deli meats. But there are serious concerns that they are carcinogenic, especially in very young children. So, buy only nitrate-free versions.

FOODS WITH TRANS FATS: Avoid foods with hydrogenated oil (of any type) on the ingredients label, or that list trans fat in the nutritional breakdown. In this case, moderation is not a good thing.

CAFFEINATED DRINKS: So you're addicted and you want to get your kid hooked, too? Although the jury is out as to how bad caffeine really is, your kids don't need it. So leave it out until he gets sucked into the habit on his own when he's older.

Okay let's do a reality check. It's not a tragedy if your child has eaten these foods. But while you can, you should present them with the best options. Research indicates that the more a person is exposed to the taste of fats, sugar, and salts, the more they crave them. If you want yourself and your child to have a taste for healthful, real foods, don't poison palates with these processed foods.

12

How to Eat

Bad eating habits can trigger poor food choices. This chapter provides a menu of ways to integrate better behaviors into your existing eating patterns.

The *Lean Mommy* plan is about breaking poor eating habits and creating healthier ones. Over the next year, and over your lifetime, adopting the small steps suggested in this and the previous chapter to improve how you already eat will be key to helping you lose your baby weight and improving your health. Plus, you'll teach your kids to enjoy food and eat the right things, but not to obsess about it.

DE-POWER FOODS

HIDE FOOD CUES: Does the chocolate need to be the first thing you see when you open a food cabinet? Is the soda positioned front and center in the fridge? Reduce temptation by hiding sometimes foods that you keep at home. If food magazines also stimulate you to eat, then get them off the coffee table!

BEWARE OF ADVERTISING: Advertisers spend hundreds of millions of dollars trying to get inside your kid's head, even at very young ages. Whenever possible, skip commercials or watch programs that don't have them.

TAKE A TIMEOUT: Much of the time we are driven to foods impulsively. Even if at that instant we think that candy would be just the thing we need, if we gave it a second thought, we might realize that, no, a sandwich might be better, or an iced tea would do the trick. So, count down for sixty seconds when you feel a craving.

SET THE TABLE: Slow eating down by laying out a placemat and cutlery on the table anytime you are going to eat, even if just for a snack.

EAT: Often we eat the worst when we are hungry or looking for something to satisfy a craving. If you stay satiated by snacking every three or four hours on cottage cheese and sunflower seeds, edamame (nutrient-rich soybeans in the shell), an apple and nuts, celery and peanut butter, or carrots and hummus, for example, you will feel less deprived and less hungry.

HYDRATE: Dehydration can be confused with hunger symptoms. Drink water to stay full.

GOOD DINING HABITS

EAT ONLY AT YOUR DINING ROOM TABLE: Don't chow down on the couch or at your desk or in the car, and definitely avoid eating in bed! Eating only at the table will reduce the triggers you feel if you've learned to associate certain foods with certain places—like munching popcorn while you watch TV, or slurping a Frappuccino while you drive your car.

USE ALL YOUR SENSES: Many diet programs make food the enemy. But food is something wonderful to be savored. Reframe your eating-is-bad paradigm and learn to enjoy food with all your senses. With each bite, eat slowly and savor the aroma, taste, texture, and sight. Eat beautiful foods with colorful palettes. Try this sensperience game with your family: Take turns feeding each other with your eyes closed. See if foods taste different. You may find that you like foods that you don't normally like, or vice versa.

STAY SATISFIED: Review the Hunger Scale readings from your food diary in Chapter 3. It's okay to feel a little hungry before your meal, but don't get ravenous. Eat or snack frequently enough, about every three hours, so that your body stays consistently fueled. At meals, try not to eat so much that you feel stuffed.

EAT MEALS AS A FAMILY: For many people, the 6:00 p.m. family dinner is a relic of the past. But eating with your kids is a valuable way to shape their eating experience. Not only can you teach them to relax and relish a good meal, you can get quality family-bonding time in. The more dysfunctional your family's eating behaviors are, the more likely it is that your children will exhibit disrupted patterns. One study found that girls who eat with the family in a structured, positive environment are less likely to exhibit disordered eating.

TAKE TWO: Most people who overeat also tend to eat too fast. During each meal, take two minutes to put your fork down. If you are eating with your family, use this as a time to brighten up the conversation. By modeling this style of eating for your children, they'll learn to relax and see a meal as a process and eating as just part of the socializing.

LEAVE A LITTLE: Let's banish the clean-plate rule once and for all! Try to not finish every bite. Even if it's just a tiny bit of cereal or a little bite of chicken, learn and teach your kids that when you are satisfied, you can stop eating. Feeling satiated should be your cue to end the meal, not an empty plate.

EATING FOR ENERGY

EAT THREE MEALS PER DAY, BUT AIM FOR FIVE: More often than not, people skip meals and eat infrequently during the day. This triggers a physiological response that encourages your body to preserve every calorie it gets and store more fat. So get in the habit of eating at regular times and in regular intervals. I know it seems counterintuitive, but eating more often may help you lose weight.

ALWAYS EAT BREAKFAST: Adults and kids who skip breakfast tend to be heavier and less productive. Missing out in the morning makes you more likely to binge later. So even if you are just eating some fruit or whole grain toast, have something to start your day.

BROWN-BAG IT: If you have a full-time job, or eat out for lunch, prepare a bagged lunch and bring it with you. You'll have complete control over what you eat, you'll save money, and you'll reduce the temptation to eat things that you wish to avoid.

DRINK UP!: Water is one of your body's most essential nutrients. Not getting enough can make a new mom tired and cranky. The best test for your fluid status is to monitor the color of your urine. If it is very yellow, the urea has not been diluted well because you are lacking H_2O. Drink enough so that you have clear or very light yellow urine. (Keep in mind that some vitamin supplements or foods can affect urine color, too.) Nursing mothers need to increase water intake even more to ensure proper hydration and successful milk production.

You get water from fluids as well as from the foods you eat. Although how much you need will vary according to your size, your diet, your activity levels, and your environment (you'll need more during hot weather), the general recommendation of getting eight 8-ounce glasses a day is a good goal.

An easy way to get your fill is to drink a glass of water when you wake up and one in the evening before you go to bed. Or carry a 64-ounce (or so) water bottle with you throughout the day. Drinking water with, or before, each meal is also a good way to curb your appetite.

If you fill up on natural, fresh foods you will maintain healthy hydration. While it's probably not a surprise that foods like lettuce, cucumbers, cabbage, broccoli, and watermelon are over 90 percent water, even fish and chicken have over 70 percent water. Processed, packaged foods usually have the water sucked out of them. Saltine crackers, for example, are only one percent water.

CUT 100 CALORIES

Any diet can help you lose weight. They may cite different reasons, but all of them are structured so that you cut out calories. Most "healthy" diets chop off around 500 calories from what you eat normally. Less healthy diets may axe 1,000 calories or more from what you eat. Talk about feeling deprived!

With either option, it's not easy to carry on this way for too long, which is why you're probably not going to stay on the diet. Eating a balanced diet full of healthy foods will get you where you want to be long-term. When you substitute more fresh foods that tend to be lower in fat and higher in fiber, as well as more nutritious, you automatically cut calories but without feeling deprived because you may actually be eating a lot more in terms of bulk. And the calories you save add up. It's the little choices that you consistently make that mean the difference between an overweight you and a Lean Mommy.

Remember, small steps add up: If all you did was modify your food and drink intake just enough to cut out 100 calories every day from your normal diet, you would lose about ten pounds in a year. Not bad for a tiny behavioral change. If you also up your calorie-burning daily, you can see how, over time, sticking to it will result in major weight loss.

Simple substitutions like changing whole milk to skim (for yourself, not your young children), decreasing the amount of sugar you add to cereal or coffee, or simply serving yourself a smaller portion of meat, potatoes, spaghetti, or cheese, can all lop off the small amount of calories that can make a big difference.

DON'T DRINK YOUR CALORIES

It's very easy for kids and adults to drink more calories than they need. And the body has a hard time regulating this intake. If you eat too much one day, your body responds to a lower hunger level so that the next day you may eat less, for an overall effect where over a week or so, your caloric intake stays consistent. Fluid calories seem to by-pass the body's regulation mechanism, so it's easy to pile on the pounds if you drink sweetened beverages. Sodas, fruit drinks, and juices are considered one of the major culprits behind the child obesity epidemic.

It's important to stay hydrated—but you may be surprised at how many calories a soda or lemonade has. Always reach for water first (it has zero calories). When you're in the mood for an ice-cold treat, here are some smart substitutions:

LIQUID CALORIES

AVOID	CHOOSE	CALORIES SAVED IN 8 OZ. GLASS
Soda or juice	Diluted juice: mix one part juice with three parts seltzer water	85
Bottled smoothie drinks	Homemade fruit smoothie made with fruit, ice, and, if desired, artificial sweetener	120
Frozen coffee drinks	Skim chocolate milk	210
Sweetened iced tea	Plain iced tea	210
Sports drinks	Low-sodium V8 or tomato juice	250
Lemonade	Sparkling mineral water with twist of lemon	130

BUY (HOME)-MADE PRE-MADE MEALS

Buying nutritious pre-made foods in the deli department, especially at whole food grocery stores, is a good idea when you're pressed for time. Sometimes, you pay a little bit extra, but it's worth it for a better quality meal. Good pre-made deli choices:

PRE-SEASONED ROASTED CHICKEN: This saves time at home because all you have to do is throw together a salad or steam up some veggies.

PRE-MADE TURKEY BURGER PATTIES: I often throw these on a nonstick skillet. Add some tasty barbecue sauce and serve with brown rice and veggies.

PRE-MADE SALMON FILET: Salmon is one of the healthiest foods.

SALAD BAR: Create a big salad from the supermarket salad bar. At home, you can add tuna and a meal is ready to eat!

PRE-CUT VEGGIES: Use these to make mealtime preparation faster. I can whip up chicken fajitas in no time with pre-cooked chicken breast strips and pre-shredded green, red, and yellow peppers.

READY-MADE PIZZA CRUSTS: Add a jar of sauce, grated cheese, and a collection of chopped vegetables.

MAKE DISHES MORE NUTRITIOUS: If you must have macaroni and cheese, add veggies such as corn and peas. Look for health food store brands that make a healthier version of boxed mac and cheese products. If you start your kids early with added vegetables, they won't know it any other way!

EAT HEALTHFULLY IN A RESTAURANT

- Do not arrive hungry! Try to have a healthy snack before you go, so that you are less likely to over-order.
- Always order a side dish of steamed vegetables, or add extra vegetables to whatever main course you choose.
- Choose dishes that contain words like: baked, broiled, grilled, poached, steamed, skinless, white meat.
- Avoid dishes that contain words like: fried, sautéed, smothered, crispy, gravy, white sauce, creamy, dark meat.
- When eating Mexican food, order a tostada, but don't eat the shell. Order a soft—not hard—chicken taco. Go for vegetarian

burritos. Ask for boiled black beans, not refried. Ask for no sour cream, or have it on the side. Limit your basket of chips to one (shared)! Or if it's too tempting, ask the waiter not to bring you chips at all.

- When eating Italian food, order angel hair pasta with tomatoes and basil, or pasta dishes with added vegetables. Avoid creamy sauces like Alfredo, and opt for olive oil, or chicken broth. Limit the bread basket or cut it out altogether.
- When ordering pizza, be selective about the meats on top and don't get the four-cheese style! Ask for less cheese, extra veggies like mushrooms, tomatoes, chiles, and peppers. Some pizza places offer arugula, spinach, artichoke hearts, and other healthy veggies—add those!
- When ordering Chinese or Asian foods, go for chicken with broccoli, or any *lean* meat mixed with plenty of veggies. Ask for steamed veggies and fish. Ask for brown rice and mix the dish with the rice to reduce calories. Stay away from crunchy noodles, fried pork, and greasy noodles.
- In any restaurant, don't be afraid to ask for substitutions.
- Consider splitting a meal or ask the waiter to bring you half and take the other half to go.

EAT HEALTHFULLY AT A FAST FOOD JOINT

You don't have to order the burger, shake, and fries at most fast food restaurants since more of them are offering more nutritious options.

PLAN BEFORE YOU GO: If you must go, order the healthiest choices. Most fast food restaurants have Web sites that provide a nutritional breakdown for all foods. Choose those lowest in fat and calories. For example, you can order a white meat chicken burrito instead of a beef taco. Or choose nutritious avocado and salsa rather than a sour-cream-filled fried burrito.

PLAN YOUR PICKUP ALONE: If you drag your kids with you, no doubt they'll be seduced by whatever cartoon character is hawking the high-fat kid's meal. So make the excursion by yourself if you can.

DON'T SUPER-SIZE IT: It sounds obvious, but if you frequent fast food establishments, make sure to only order the regular portion and not be tempted to super-size (even if it's just a few cents more).

SKIP THE EXTRAS: Just passing on the dressing, cheese, or mayo can add up to significant caloric differences. Consider substituting fries with a side salad. (But watch out for creamy dressings and high-calorie croutons.)

MUST PASS: Whenever possible, pass on the French fries, onion rings, fried fish sandwiches, and chicken nuggets.

MAKING HEALTHY LUNCHES

Whether you're sending your two-year-old to day care, or your older child to school, the junk that some people feed their kids in lunch boxes is frightening! Some children are literally loaded down with sugary fruit packs, juice drinks, and high-fat and/or processed chips. You want your kids to have energy and be able to focus at school, so why would you hurt them with a brown bag filled with junk? If you pack up nutrient-rich meals, while they may not eat all of it, what they do eat will be good for them. And, hey, they might eat all of it and enjoy it! Here are some smart lunch items:

PACKING GREAT LUNCHES

REMOVE FROM LUNCH BOXES	INCLUDE IN LUNCH BOXES
Bologna	Turkey
Potato chips	Celery and peanut butter
Cookies	Yogurt squeeze

(continued on next page)

REMOVE FROM LUNCH BOXES	INCLUDE IN LUNCH BOXES
Sweetened iced tea	Water
Soda	Milk
White bread	Whole grain bread, tortilla, or pita
Goldfish and other crackers	Whole grain crackers without hydrogenated oils
Candy	Carrots and ranch dressing
Donuts	Raisins
Buttery popcorn	Air-popped popcorn
Licorice	Unsweetened apple sauce
Cupcakes	Any fruit (fresh or dried)
Packaged cracker and cheese	Whole grain pretzels with hummus
Fruit snacks (not real fruit)	Edamame
Pop-Tarts	Veggie sticks

It's a wonder that so much salt, fat, and processed junk could fit in any child's lunch box. If you start your children off eating the healthier options, they will not only know it but like it.

tip:

Buy plain yogurt and fruit it yourself. Flavored yogurt has become one of the all-time favorites of today's kids. Yogurt in itself is a great food. It is easier to digest than milk and has a host of good bacteria that promote good health. However, the flavored yogurts often have more sugar than a piece of candy.

MAKE HEALTHY FAST FOOD

While you may be tempted by the drive-through or a frozen dinner, you can make healthier meals in just ten minutes. And best of all, you control the ingredients. Once you get the hang of it, you won't need to take time measuring or assembling complicated meals. Here are some ideas for fast, nutritious meals:

ONE MEAL SPAGHETTI: Brown some lean ground turkey in a nonstick frying pan. When browned, throw in frozen chopped spinach, a can of chopped tomatoes, and even some grated carrots. Pour a jar of spaghetti sauce over the top. Cook up whole grain spaghetti and serve together. Sprinkle a little bit of Parmesan over for extra flavor. (Buy fresh Parmesan cheese rather than the processed canned stuff. It has a stronger flavor and a little goes a long way.)

CHICKEN BURRITOS: Buy a roasted chicken. Pull off the skin and hand-pull some pieces into bite-sized chunks. Warm up some whole wheat tortillas. Create a burrito bar where your family can assemble their own burritos. Ingredients should include pinto beans or black beans, lettuce, tomatoes, salsa, grated cheddar cheese, and the chicken.

SALMON BURGERS: Remove skin from a salmon filet and finely chop in a food processor. Add in whole wheat bread crumbs, egg, ½ cup finely chopped onion, and a dash of ginger and a squeeze of lemon juice. Mix well and mold into patties. Mist nonstick pan with olive oil spray and cook salmon patties. Serve on top of brown rice and with steamed veggies. Canned salmon can be substituted.

VEGGIE PIZZA: Use a ready-made pizza crust from the market (preferably whole wheat) or make your own. Spread dough into a large pizza circle. Top with jarred spaghetti sauce and any or all of

tip:

If your kid hates vegetables, mix them into your main meal.

the following toppings: mushrooms, red or green peppers, fresh tomatoes, broccoli, red onions, artichoke hearts, olives, baby spinach, basil. You can top it with chunks of chicken or seafood. Sprinkle with a little mozzarella cheese and bake at about 400 degrees until browned and bubbly. A pizza stone greatly improves the crust of the pizza.

COLORFUL QUESADILLA: A quesadilla is melted cheese between two tortillas. In this version, it's healthier. Put one tortilla down as the base (preferably whole grain). Layer shredded chicken, chopped veggies, and jack cheese. Top with the other tortilla. Spray a nonstick pan with a little olive oil. Brown on each side and make sure the inside is hot and melted. Serve with guacamole and salsa.

APPLE TURKEY MEATBALLS: Mix 1 grated apple, 2 tbsp Dijon mustard, 1 package ground turkey, ½ cup apricot jam, ½ cup whole wheat bread crumbs, 1 egg, and ½ cup defrosted, drained chopped spinach. Form into balls and fry in nonstick pan that has been sprayed with a little bit of oil. Sauté until browned and cooked through. Serve with quinoa (a wonderful and unique grain) and a side salad. Make bite-sized meatballs. Kids love them!

ONE POT CHILI: Chili can be one of the healthiest meals. Brown one package of lean ground turkey meat in a pot. Throw in 2 cans of beans (I like to use a variety). Add ½ cup chopped onion, 1 cup chopped spinach, and a can of chopped tomatoes. Throw in your own chili spices or use a packaged variety. So long as you watch sodium intake regularly, using this once in a while shouldn't hurt. Serve with a side salad.

LOLLIPOP CHICKEN: My friend and chef Karishma came up with this recipe because kids love food on a stick. Compared to the traditional hot dog, this grilled chicken option is healthier (and tastier). Buy a package of large lollipop sticks (can be found at most art supply stores). Skewers will work, too. Season chicken with salt and pepper. Remove the sinew or tendon. In one bowl, mix up some flour seasoned with salt and pepper. In the other bowl mix up 2 eggs and 2 tbsp water. And in the third bowl, mix up some panko breadcrumbs and a sprinkling of Parmesan cheese. Dip the chicken in the flour, then the water mixture, and then the breadcrumbs, shaking off excess in between. Fry chicken in a nonstick skillet with just a bit of oil until it is browned on each side and cooked through. Skewer onto the lollipop sticks and serve with a cooked vegetable.

SWEET POTATO SALAD: Cut sweet potatoes in French fry–type slices. Spray lightly with olive oil and sprinkle with salt and pepper. Bake at 425 degrees for 30 minutes or until tender. Mix sweet potatoes with 2 tbsp of apple cider vinegar and 1 tbsp olive oil. Sprinkle chopped scallions throughout. Serve warm or cold.

KASHI FRUIT AMBROSIA: Cook one packet of Kashi as directed on box. Mix cooked Kashi with your choice of fruit. Stir in ½ cup plain yogurt and ¼ cup honey or brown sugar.

HEALTHY TORTILLA CHIPS: Cut corn tortilla in triangles. Put on baking sheet. Spray lightly with olive oil and sprinkle with salt (and/or other seasonings). Bake at 400 degrees until crisp and lightly browned.

VEGGIE LASAGNA: Layer the following: Whole wheat lasagna noodles, chopped spinach, shredded carrots, chopped tomatoes, chopped bell peppers, ricotta, and mozzarella. Want some more protein? Shred some cooked chicken and add to the mix. Bake at 350 degrees for about 30 minutes.

> **tip:**
>
> Kale is one of the most nutritious greens around. Wash and dry it and tear it up into pieces. Put it in a bag and freeze it. I throw a few handfuls into our smoothies. The taste is barely noticeable but the benefits are immense.

CHAPTER **13**

Be an Opti-Mom

To be the best mom you can be, you owe it to your family to put your health first. Taking me-time is not being selfish. Your whole family will flourish if you are happier and less stressed. Plus your kids will learn your healthy behaviors. This chapter shows you how to make and model positive choices.

Who hasn't chuckled the first time they saw their toddler imitate the way mom or dad talks on the phone? But who is still smiling when the child pretends to smoke one of daddy's cigarettes—or when cutie spews out the same curse words you flung at the truck driver that cut you off two days ago?

Kids are like sponges and they take in more than the ABCs, shapes, and colors that you teach them. The fact is that your child is watching—and mimicking—your every move. And that's why treating yourself well by not only living healthfully but by communicating positive thoughts about your own body is crucial. Do you want your child to suffer from the body image issues that you may grapple with? Your most important job as mom is not changing diapers; it's shaping how your child views herself and impacting the lifestyle habits that she will adopt.

YOU ARE "ON" EVEN WHEN YOU ARE "OFF"

Most parents try to be on their best behavior around their kids—keeping arguing publicly to a minimum, stressing values like honesty, and teaching good manners. But kids are still on during off moments when you're in a hurry or on the phone. Many moms aren't aware of how powerful their off-the-record behavior is. But if mom puts down her thunder thighs or fat tummy, guess who else will, too? A verbalized feeling-fat moment while stepping on the scale teaches a child something that she should never have been exposed to: that there is a "right" and a "wrong" way for his or her body to be. The child loves mom and at a young age would not notice her flaws. But mom's comment now zooms the child's attention to the idea that, as great as she is, mommy doesn't like herself or her body. This makes her child hyperaware of his or her own body. And he or she learns to judge their own body negatively, too.

Does this sound familiar? You go to a playgroup where the kids are playing and the moms chat among themselves. Talk ranges from gossip about someone's new boobs to the latest diet you are trying. Don't fool yourself. They can hear you!

It never ceases to amaze me when moms ask for advice on their children's eating problems. I ask the mom to keep a food diary of her own eating patterns. She'll always get defensive, explaining that it's her child that has the issues. But it

THINGS THAT MAKE ME GO HMMMMM

Here are real-life examples from my Stroller Strides classes:

Kate gave her fifteen-month-old child a Peppermint Pattie. She noticed my shocked look. "She *loves* these and can't get enough of them," the mom explained. Hello? Why was this child ever introduced to a Peppermint Pattie in the first place? At fifteen months, you have total control over what your child is exposed to. Your child might love wine, but you wouldn't give her that just because she wanted it, would you?

Vicky's child was in the stroller, her fingers busy in the snack tray. "What's that?" I asked. "It's edamame," her mommy said. "She loves squeezing them from their shells." Now that's what I call introducing your child to all kinds of foods!

Elizabeth brought her five-year-old to class. He asked her for his candy. Out came a package of dried prunes. He was excited and gobbled them right up. *That's* what he thought was candy. Interesting!

never fails. Once I examine her habits, it's usually mom that has disordered eating: She's always on diets, doesn't eat with her family, or serves her family different food than she eats. The messages learned from mom are that food can be bad, eating can be a battlefield, or that bingeing can be used to deal with emotion.

Kids should learn that eating is a wonderful experience and that food fuels your body. But if you are not living the way you want your kids to live, they will not learn the positive attitudes. That's why if you make life-affirming lifestyle choices for yourself, then you will really be a model mommy. I call this type of mother an Opti-Mom. An Opti-Mom chooses healthy foods, is physically active every day, and models positive attitudes.

TALK LIKE AN OPTI-MOM

Everything from a loud pronouncement to a little comment said under your breath will affect your child. Both your words and actions will have a powerful effect on the way your children think about and treat themselves, and how they think about and treat others for their entire lives. Here are some examples of both negative and positive self-talk. Keep in mind that you may not always believe the Opti-Mom message you are conveying. But for now, that doesn't matter. It's your responsibility to transmit positive messages to your child. So if you have to fake it in order to do so, then that's what you need to do. The more you act like you love your body or the more often you adopt a positive mind-set, you may actually start to believe yourself.

> "LISA has made me hyperaware of how much we talk about our bodies, food, and diets in front of our children. I am taken aback by how often she has to stop us in our tracks in our conversations. I want my two girls to feel comfortable with their bodies and their health."
>
> —HEATHER HEGGIE, 35,
> mom of Sara, 4, Luke, 2, Hannah, 1 week

SITUATION: You just came home from the gym and are telling your husband about your workout.

NEGATIVE-MOM TALK: "I'm so glad I got that over with. I was bored out of my skull on the treadmill."

OPTI-MOM TALK: "I feel energized after my workout. I had a great run!"

SITUATION: You're eating at a picnic with friends and someone offers you some coleslaw with mayo in it.

NEGATIVE-MOM TALK: "Oh I can't eat that, it's way too fattening."

OPTI-MOM TALK: "No thank you. I'm really craving those juicy tomatoes."

SITUATION: Your child wants to know why he can't have dinosaur-shaped fried chicken tonight like his friend does.

NEGATIVE-MOM TALK: "We only eat healthy things in this house. I won't let you eat that junk."

OPTI-MOM TALK: "It's great for you to have that as a treat when you go to his house. We all make different kinds of foods. Would you like to make Lollipop Chicken tonight [see recipe on pages 182–183]? I bet your friend would like to try that at our house one night."

ACT LIKE AN OPTI-MOM

Actions speak louder than words. A kid can see right through a double standard: mom saying one thing and doing another. So keep on your toes and make sure that your behavior is reinforcing what you want your child to learn.

Promise now: Never say anything negative about your body, your children's, or anyone else's in front of your kids.

SITUATION: You're in the dressing room at the store trying on a pair of pants.

NEGATIVE-MOM ACTION: You turn around and look at your butt in the mirror and grimace.

OPTI-MOM ACTION: You look at yourself in the mirror, stand proudly, and look without distress.

SITUATION: You truly do need to lose some weight and are planning a new eating plan for yourself.

NEGATIVE-MOM ACTION: You don't eat meals with your kids and/or you eat packaged or diet foods in front of your family.

OPTI-MOM ACTION: You include the foods you need on the table along with whatever else you will serve your family. Everyone chooses what they want. You moderate your portions, but you do not bring attention to your "dieting."

THE 11 COMMANDMENTS TO BE AN OPTI-MOM

TURN OFF THE TV

TV is a mom's easiest way out. But even though kids' shows are doing a better job at promoting healthy foods and fitness now that obesity has become a national crisis, your kids are still blasted with hours of advertising designed to get them to want, crave (and beg) for highly processed, sugary, salty, fattening junk foods. Research shows that the more hours they spend glued to the set, the more overweight they tend to be.

TEACH YOUR CHILD TO COOK

When you eat healthfully, so does your child. When they eat healthfully, so do you! Get your children involved in cooking early. A toddler can sit on the floor with the mixing bowl and a spoon. As they get older, they can help mix and pour (and clean up!). If you have space to garden, grow vegetables. They are more excited to eat when they contribute to the finished meal.

DON'T FORCE FOOD

It's human nature to want what you can't have. Jacob became picky at four and would no longer eat vegetables that he used to eat.

Explaining that vegetables were full of vitamins would not do the trick. So I would prepare myself veggies, but not serve any to him. "Why didn't you give me any?" he would ask. "Oh, I can't give you these," I said. "These will make you way too strong and I'm not ready for you to be strong like a superhero yet." "I want them," he would say, and gobble them all up. I have never forced my children to eat or finish anything. Ellyn Satter, M.S., R.D. author of *Child of Mine*, suggests that *your* job is to provide healthy well-rounded meals to your children at set times throughout the day. *Their* job is to decide what to eat and how much to eat.

EXPOSE THEM TO THE BEST (NOT THE REST)

Animal babies learn to eat from watching their moms, and so do human babies. What you feed your child determines what he'll like and crave. In fact, a baby's tastes may begin *early*. Research has shown that babies exposed to a variety of foods during pregnancy are more likely to be open to new foods later. And flavors such as garlic, carrot, mint, and vanilla have been found to be transmitted through breast milk. One study found that babies exposed to carrot flavor from breastfeeding were more likely than those not exposed to accept carrots later. Breastfed babies may be less picky as kids (and into adulthood) than formula-fed infants, especially if their moms eat a balanced diet while nursing.

When your child starts eating solid foods, why give a processed chicken nugget over tasty grilled chicken? A sweet crunchy apple may not feel like a treat to you, but it is to your child if you present it that way. A study of more than 3,000 kids under age two found that many had already developed an appetite for hot dogs, French fries, candy, and soda. This is disconcerting since these preferences will probably be with them through life.

While you shouldn't verbally condemn foods, you should offer natural, wholesome food *most* of the time, and *especially* at home. Jacob, who is now five, has never had soda because he's never been exposed to it yet. He's also not used to artificially flavored and/or super-sweet snacks. So when he's at a birthday party, he rarely finishes his cake. It's so sweet that a little bit is plenty. You can shape your kids' tastes when they are young. They don't *need* sodas, candy, super-sweet juice drinks, processed items packaged with cartoon characters, or sugary cereals. Your child will have plenty of time to be exposed to junk.

BEWARE OF GETTING DEFENSIVE

It's natural to feel resistant to these suggestions. You may protest: *I grew up on cake and Kool-Aid. If my parents had donuts every Sunday, what's so bad about carrying on the tradition?* True, a little junk never hurt anyone. And we don't want to ban and, therefore, deprive kids of foods. That gives these foods power and may make them crave those foods more. Your house should be filled with fun, plentiful food choices, not seen as the house that has nothing good to eat.

We should make it easy for our kids to *want* to eat a healthier food. Isn't that *our* problem in the first place? We crave the junk and therefore succumb to it—and then justify it ("a little in moderation is okay"). If we didn't want it in the first place it would be easier to avoid. From a nutritional standpoint, foods such as donuts or pure-sugar drinks provide no benefit. So why train our kids to splurge with them?

If you eat poorly most of the time, healthier foods may seem bland in comparison because processed foods are chemically modified to have strong, possibly addictive flavors. If you crave sodas or fast food, you can train yourself to make healthier choices by allowing time to get used to new tastes. If we provide an environment where a child grows used to healthier foods, good food seems tastier and the junk isn't as enticing. Do what's in the best long-term interests of your child. The point of this book is that you, too, will benefit from the healthier choices you model for your children.

DON'T GLORIFY JUNK FOOD

It may be unrealistic to ban all the "good stuff" from the house. What happens if either you or your husband comes down with a late-night candy bar craving? Eat it when your child is not around. Or keep your portion sensible and minimize its importance. You may be savoring every succulent slurp of that chocolate shake, but treat it like a glass of iced tea in front of your child, instead of a prized reward—it's just a food, after all.

DON'T TREAT BOREDOM WITH FOOD

It's amazing how early we use food as a tool. If you are a first-time mom, you are hypersensitive to your baby crying. You feel that you must do whatever will make him or her happy. Sometimes that means holding the baby, but we soon realize that a snack will stifle almost any whine. When our kids are cranky or bored, we toss them a teething biscuit or Cheerios.

"I feel better mentally and physically. I'm a better wife and mother because of Stroller Strides."

—DEENA SACKS PRICHARD, 32,
mom of Maia, 3,
Nashville, Tennessee

Stop! Think about it. You've just taught your six-month-old that food will alleviate boredom or angst. If your child is not actually hungry, let her figure out how to entertain herself in more positive ways like looking for bugs in the backyard or tumbling in the living room.

LABEL FOOD AND FITNESS IN A POSITIVE WAY

Food doesn't have to be a battle. Exercise doesn't have to be something that must be endured. Establish these negative associations if you want your child to grow up into an adult who *forces* himself to live healthfully (like we do). But if you want to help your child be active and eat well for life, then make food good and exercise an adventure.

I give Jacob a vegetable juice concoction made of greens, bananas, pineapple juice, and wheat germ that I call "Incredible Hulk juice." Other kids would run away from this green smoothie. But Jake thinks he'll be an action hero if he drinks it, so he loves it! And when Jake incessantly asks me to play tag, my gut reaction after a twelve-hour day is to say, "No, mommy is too tired." His interpretation to that is that exercise will make me more tired. The funny thing is that when I (make myself) say "Yes!," we have a great time getting completely out of breath and laughing. The truth is that I feel much more energized after playing than I do when we start. (Oh yeah, aren't I supposed to know that exercise will give you energy?)

NEVER DISPARAGE YOURSELF OR OTHERS

Fat bias is perhaps the one prejudice still alive and uncontested in our politically correct culture. But even if you feel it, you must not perpetuate it. We are the generation of moms that must stop the cycle of body-bashing so that our kids (and their kids) grow up in a more supporting, empowering society. Avoid commenting when you feel fat or when other people look fat. There's no reason to create negative associations for your children. If you slip, turn it around into a positive, empowering comment.

It upsets me to hear a mom call her healthy child overweight. Many of us fear our children being fat as if it's a reflection on us. It's only when you present negative eating behaviors or create a lifestyle of sedentary living (lots of TV) that a child won't be able to regulate his weight. Please, mommies, do not lay your own weight concerns on your child. Children exposed to physical activity and healthful foods will eat and exercise as they should. Highly active children will stay at a healthy weight.

FIND CREATIVE WAYS TO CALM DOWN

It's a running joke that women escape to a pint of Häagen-Dazs for emotional support. The last thing we need to do is ingrain this message—or behavior—in our kids. We should not only learn to confront and communicate feelings, we should present a healthy solution when soothing is needed. So if you're trying to entice your

"I always struggled with my weight and was a little obsessive. But through Stroller Strides I've learned to give myself a little breathing room and take a day off if I need to."

—MERI TREITLER, 32,
mom of Jake, 2,
New York, New York

child out of a temper tantrum, don't offer a cookie or his favorite video. Instead, suggest going for a bike ride or putting special bubbles in the bath. Demonstrate your own positive coping mechanisms, too. (Your child is watching.) Discuss problems calmly and rationally with your husband or friends. Or go for an invigorating jog.

KEEP HUBBY IN LINE

Sometimes your husband thwarts your efforts. He arrives home with a super-sized soda and a giant bag of potato chips. Or he sniggers about "health food." And there's nothing like the dad who takes the child to a kid-friendly fast food restaurant just to score extra points over mom!

mommy meditation #3

Sit in a quiet upright position. Breathe quietly and visualize yourself enacting a habit or behavior that you would like to change. Just pick one. Picture yourself participating in this behavior and then envision the consequences if you continue with it. Slowly focus on the effects of this behavior at moments in time: Linger on today, imagine it tomorrow, picture an outcome if you are still doing it next week. Portray yourself in ten years of repeating this pattern: How will it have affected you, your friends, or your family? And finally create the picture of how you would be if you continued till the end of your life. Would there have been an effect on your relationships? On your health? Notice whether this behavior at any stage interferes with your happiness. If what you see pains you, linger longer. Allow yourself to feel the full force of your potentially self-destructive habit.

If your husband dampens your enthusiasm, even in jest, your child may side with dad in the subtle power game at play. That's why you should educate your husband on why you are making the food and fitness choices that you do. Even if he is not ready to revamp his own lifestyle, he'll probably be responsive to at least modeling better behavior in front of the kids. Most dads want to do the best for their children.

14

Troubleshooting Tough Times

In a perfect world, you'd eat the best things and exercise every day. But life happens. The kids get sick. You get sick. Your computer crashes. The car goes on the blink. This chapter shows you ways to cope when the going gets tough.

Adherence to a plan, not the program itself, is the most important determinant in success. No matter how perfect your diet or exercise routine is, if you don't follow through and make it a part of your daily life, you simply won't get results. Period.

Your ability to stick with a plan is influenced by many factors. Beginners are more likely to drop out, as are those who don't make their goal a priority. And most importantly, people who are rigid and unable to adapt to changing circumstances in their lives are more likely to let their commitment fall by the wayside. Recognize that, at times, you may need to do less than you'd hoped, or make a so-so choice instead of the ideal one. The typical person throws in the towel when she slips up. But if you make modifications when your life calls for it, you will stay on course and reach your goal. Here are common stumbling blocks—and how to maneuver around them.

STUMBLING BLOCK: BABY BLUES

If you are starting to question whether having a baby was the right thing to do, or whether you're prepared to be a mom, or even whether you love your child, you may have postnatal depression. There are different levels that can range from just feeling in a funk to losing your sense of purpose and feeling completely overwhelmed. Many women who left a career to have a child often feel lost when suddenly all they are doing is taking care of this new foreign body. Since life does drastically change, especially after your first child, it's not always easy to tell a true case of the baby blues from a period of shock and adjustment to a whole new way of life. Of course, at its most severe, a mom may become so depressed that she neglects her child, or even wants to hurt him or herself.

Nursing can also present problems. Not many people realize beforehand just how difficult nursing can be. It's *supposed* to be so natural, but some babies won't latch on or seem uninterested. Also, nursing can hurt. Many women eventually get it with the help of a professional. Others who don't can often feel incompetent. If you're depressed, the last thing you feel like doing is taking care of yourself with exercise and good nutrition.

STICK-WITH-IT STRATEGIES

Many moms are socially isolated the first few months of baby's life because they've been told by the doctor to avoid exposing him to germs. But that loss of empathetic mom-friends can magnify feelings of sadness and isolation. If you are experiencing any unusually sad feelings, speak to your doctor and/or a therapist—especially if you are having any destructive thoughts. Postpartum depression is not uncommon, but if it's serious and left untreated it can put you or your baby at risk. If you are just in the doldrums, one of the first things that doctors recommend is to exercise. All the feel-good effects can lift your spirits. Also, get more sleep. If you're a first-time mom, you might feel compelled to be there every time your baby wakes up. But help yourself and baby by letting your husband take a shift so you can get a solid block of shut-eye.

Food may also affect your mood. The more junk you eat, the less well nourished you'll be and that affects all the physiological functions in the cells throughout your body. So try to eat fresh fruit and vegetables, fish, lean meats and poultry, and beans and whole grains. See Chapter 12 for easy ways to integrate better eating habits.

STUMBLING BLOCK: A FRIEND OR FAMILY MEMBER DRAGS YOU DOWN

We're motivated by the people around us. The new you may make family, friends, or co-workers feel uncomfortable or threatened. Even though unintentional, they can sabotage your weight management efforts with a negative or sarcastic remark that deflates your confidence. A strong support system, on the other hand, will help keep you motivated with positive reinforcement. Recognize who helps, and who impedes, your efforts.

THE DRAINER: Some people are negative and absolutely drain you. You know the ones. They always have a problem, an ache or a pain. They are probably going nowhere themselves and would like you to stay for the ride.

THE PERSISTENT PESSIMIST: Some people have a negative influence, but you're stuck with them (they are part of your family or work environment).

THE MOTIVATOR: This person is always looking at the bright side. You feel energy and inspiration to be better when you're with them.

STICK-WITH-IT STRATEGIES

You need people around who will support you. So you may need to get choosy about whom you associate with.

STAY CLEAR OF THE DRAINER: (You don't need to let them know—take an extra few days to return phone calls, avoid scheduling visits, and so on.) These people have little to give you right now and can thwart your good efforts. It doesn't mean that they won't be part of your life again, but it helps to keep distance when you are in a vulnerable stage trying to make important lifestyle changes.

KEEP AN EMOTIONAL DISTANCE FROM THE PERSISTENT PESSIMIST: You may have to interact with them, but be aware of their effect on you and avoid letting them influence your feelings. Plan ahead when you know you will spend time with them. Put up a barrier so that you don't let them get you down.

INVITE MOTIVATORS INTO YOUR LIFE: They're hard to find, so hunt them out and keep them in your life forever! These people tend to give back at least as much as they take. (Pssst! The best way to find these people is to be one of them yourself.)

TEACH FRIENDS AND FAMILY TO HELP: Often, people don't realize that they are undermining you. Make them aware, but avoid being confrontational by sharing your goals. Reassure them that just because you are changing your habits doesn't mean that they have to also. Ask for their positive reinforcement. For example, let them know that you're trying to eat at the table and ask them to commend you when you do. But make it clear that you don't want them yelling at you when you eat at your desk or on the couch.

FIND LIKE-MINDED SUPPORT GROUPS: Perhaps the biggest reason why Stroller Strides has helped—and continues to help—so many moms is that it provides an always available support group for those who feel no one understands what they are going through. The multiple minds and hearts at work in a group mean that when you are not thinking rationally or feel out of control, others can give clear, sensible advice. Groups provide comfort through shared experiences. You'll learn how others have handled similar challenges and you'll make one another feel less isolated. Often, just talking about a problem helps give you perspective and organize your thoughts. When someone keeps troubled feelings inside, a problem can get magnified and seem much bigger than it really is.

Look for a Stroller Strides group near you at www.stroller strides.com. If this is not feasible, find a local support group or playgroup in your area.

STUMBLING BLOCK: AN UNHEALTHY HISTORY WITH FOOD OR EATING DISORDERS

Women who've had issues with disordered eating behaviors, or even a full-blown eating disorder like anorexia or bulimia, may find that they regain control while pregnant and can eat normally for their growing baby. But afterward, the disordered behavior can resurface.

STICK-WITH-IT STRATEGY

A few tips here are not sufficient since the psychological aspects involved must be explored. If you are having trouble with these issues, see a therapist. Not only is your health at risk, but you are highly likely to pass your disordered thought patterns and warped body image on to your children. So make an appointment with a therapist *now*.

STUMBLING BLOCK: CONSTANT FOOD CRAVINGS

Do problem foods get you every time? Cookies are one of my trigger foods. In the past, if I was tired, stressed, or feeling overwhelmed, I could open the cabinet, see cookies, and eat them without thinking until the whole box was gone.

STICK-WITH-IT STRATEGIES

LEGALIZE THE FOOD: We give foods power when we make them forbidden. And denial drives many women to a point where they are trying so hard not to eat a certain food that they subconsciously focus on it so much that they are compelled to have it. Or they splurge on something else. They pressure themselves to be "good," but then when they are "bad" they cheat big-time.

An old boyfriend of mine once ate an entire quart of Häagen-Dazs ice cream while we were watching TV. And it didn't bother him in the least. I couldn't so much as look at a scoop without thinking that it was taboo. If I had eaten what he ate, I would have lamented for hours about how I binged. His nonreaction made me contemplate our differences. *Why was it a binge for me and a treat for him?*

Binge-eating is defined as uncontrollable eating where a person rapidly consumes an excessive amount of food. This guy didn't eat rapidly. He savored his ice cream while watching a movie. And it wasn't a big deal—he was generally a healthy eater and exercised regularly. For him, it was a treat—but without a label and emotion attached to it. I realized that because I labeled ice cream as "bad" and not allowed, I gave the food control over me. This makes it more desirable and so when you succumb to it, you may binge because you know you won't allow yourself to eat it again.

However, if you believe that you can have any food anytime—and you *truly believe* that you can—then you'll not feel a need to overindulge: You know you can have it again. And even if you do (hey, sometimes something just tastes really good), the body has a way of compensating. Normally, physiological mechanisms regulate energy intake. If you overeat one day, you will naturally be less hungry and eat less the next day or two. It's okay to eat ice cream, pizza, or chocolate occasionally if, most of the time, you choose healthier foods.

MAKE IT HARD-TO-GET: Curb impulsive reactions by slowing down the process. A little time to think and consider your actions and options may be all you need to realize that you don't really want it, or that the downsides are not worth it. So, not buying or, if you do, putting trigger foods in a hard-to-get-to location can put on the brakes.

MAKE IT LESS TEMPTING: Sometimes you can obtain the same texture or flavor in a healthier way. I used to be addicted to processed peanut butter. I could shovel it in by the spoonful. I decided to switch to the all-natural kind. The pure peanut butter is good, but doesn't have the same dessertlike appeal. So I get the taste. But a little is enough. I also buy whole grain, organic cookies. True, they don't have the same zip as an Oreo, but they are better for me and still give the cookie feel. After years of educating myself about foods, I now view processed cookies with disgust. How could I put something with about a million chemicals into my body? I have changed my thought process so that I don't want it anymore. You can, too!

GIVE YOURSELF OPTIONS: Have you ever looked for food in a gas station mini-mart? Your only choices are candy, chips, sodas, and processed bakery items. If you're hungry enough, you'll take whatever there is. Keep your pantry, car, and diaper bag stocked with healthy nibbles. That way you never feel like there is nothing to eat, and you are less likely to succumb to junk.

AIM FOR 80/20: With exercise or good eating, it's what we do—and stick to—most of the time that makes the difference. If the thought of having to be perfect is too intimidating, follow the 80/20 rule where you make healthy choices 80 percent of the time and allow yourself your indulgences 20 percent of the time. So you might decide that every Sunday you'll have dessert, but during the week you'll go for fruit. Or if you're going out for a heavy meal, balance it out by eating lighter foods the rest of the day.

STUMBLING BLOCK: STRESS-EATING WHEN YOU ARE NOT HUNGRY

Most people overeat because of emotional triggers. So plan how you will deal with stress.

STICK-WITH-IT STRATEGIES

GET ACTIVE: Your body reacts to stress by releasing hormones like adrenaline and cortisol that raise your heart rate and blood pressure and give you a boost of energy so that you may either fight or flee the stressful situation. Cortisol also acts as an appetite stimulant to replenish the energy lost during the fight-or-flight response. However, most of us are not able to literally fight or flee a situation, so we're left with surges in stress hormones. Exercise naturally counters the physical effects of stress on your body, and it also helps boost your mental outlook. So when you feel overwhelmed, go on a bicycle ride, walk, garden, dance, or clean the house. If you're at work when stress hits, take a quick walk or a stretch break. You'll handle your stress in a way that automatically makes you stick with your *Lean Mommy* program.

DO A MOMMY MEDITATION: We're busy morning, noon, and night. So there is not a lot of quiet time in our heads. When you need a mental cool-down, find a quiet space for a few minutes. Sit upright, either on the floor with your legs crossed or straight in front of you, or in a chair with your feet flat on the floor. Rest your hands on your legs and turn your palms out so that they face the ceiling. Touch your thumb and forefinger together. Close your eyes and form a mental picture of the flow of your breath. With your eyes closed, focus on watching the flow as it streams into your nostrils and out into the air. Try to maneuver the air flow so that it streams through just one nostril at a time. Then revert to breathing out of both nostrils but try to balance the amount of oxygen coming in through each. Sit and focus on your breathing for five minutes.

If you start your day with a Mommy Meditation, or establish a set time each day, you'll be amazed at how calm you feel during the rest of the day. You'll find different Mommy Meditations to try scattered throughout the book.

CREATE POSITIVE ASSOCIATIONS: Changing your outlook isn't easy. Rather than think of a run on the treadmill as tedious, remind yourself how invigorating it is. Tell yourself over and over. Or look for the positive aspects of a spinach salad. Yum: crunchy, green, fresh, light!

STUMBLING BLOCK: NOT A SECOND TO SPARE

One of the most common excuses for not exercising or eating properly is not having enough time. There is no question that with a new baby, you may be at one of the busiest points in your life.

STICK-WITH-IT STRATEGIES

Putting off what you need to do for your health won't help. If you view your own well-being as necessary, you'll make it a priority. You brush your teeth every day, don't you? This is a behavior that you don't even question—partly because you experience immediate negative repercussions if you don't (bad breath). And you are aware of the long-term side effects like cavities and gum disease. With exercise and eating well, the immediate effects of not doing it aren't always obvious—especially if you have not been doing them. But not only will poor habits catch up with you, you need to model behaviors (positive exercise and eating) well for your kids. So don't make them an option, figure out how to fit them in.

DON'T CALL IT EXERCISE: Find a way to fit a walk into your schedule. Or go to a Stroller Strides session and call it a playgroup. Find a way to be active in a way that doesn't feel like it's a drain on your time.

KEEP IT SIMPLE: If you don't have time to organize child care, go to Stroller Strides or join a neighbor for a stroller walk on your own. Or have hubby baby-sit and instead of a lengthy gym visit, just step outside your door for a quick jog. Or close yourself off in a room with a fitness video or DVD.

KEEP HEALTHY READY-TO-EAT FOODS ON HAND: When you're feeling frantic, the last thing you're going to do is prepare an elaborate meal. So prepare in advance ready-to-eat healthy foods. Wash all fruit and vegetables as soon as you buy them and prep them to be eaten: Cut little clumps of grapes so you can grab a few easily, have baby carrots in sight, display fruit, rather than hiding it in the recesses of your refrigerator, keep slices of low-fat cheese in a Baggie ready to nibble on, have edamame pre-steamed in a bowl. And al-

"I was a cheerleader in high school and in great shape. But when I got pregnant, I lost all control and lived on McDonald's and chocolate and gained sixty-five pounds. After having the baby, I was tired all the time because I was a single mom working two jobs to survive. But so far I've lost about forty pounds because I've learned to prepare my foods the night before so that I don't order fast food, and I sacrifice a little sleep to wake up early and work out."

—STEPHANIE FELION, 21, mom of Jeremiah Washington, 2, Portland, Oregon

ways carry nuts, whole grain pretzels, or dried fruit in your diaper bag or purse.

STUMBLING BLOCK: MENTALLY EXHAUSTED

Juggling a full-time job with home and mom duties can be challenging—especially if colleagues or your boss aren't exactly sympathetic. It's easy to think that you don't deserve—and can't possibly muster up the energy—to fit in exercise.

STICK-WITH-IT STRATEGY

Sometimes it is better to take the pressure off and wait for when the timing is right to embark upon a new regimen. But that doesn't mean that you can't still live a *Lean Mommy* lifestyle in a more relaxed way. Remember, it's the little things that you do consistently over time that will make a difference in the long run. So, rather than trying to improve on too many habits at once, make a few subtle changes such as using one less teaspoon of sugar or nixing the blue cheese dressing on your daily salad and using lemon juice and a splash of olive oil instead. Browse through Chapter 12 for easy ways to integrate smart changes into your eating patterns.

CHAPTER 15

Your LEAN Future

A woman came up to me recently and said, "I may not be at my thinnest or lowest weight, but I am strong and I am healthy. Plus, I have the energy to carry my two kids around all day and to play Frisbee with them." I gave her a big hug: That, to me, is what it is all about. And it hit me—you so rarely hear a comment like this from women. We don't let ourselves say, You know, I'm okay with my weight right now. We should be able to graduate to the point where we can be appreciative of our bodies right now, no matter what.

If I could get all women to embrace health for themselves and to focus on balance and wellness, and in doing so set the stage for the next generation, I'd consider that an incredible legacy. Right now, our kids are set up for either obesity or eating disorders. Our kids' generation is predicted to have a lower life expectancy than our own! And unless we rise up as a movement of mothers willing to change ourselves to help our kids, then the cycle we see is bound to get worse. We need to change the social pressure to be thin and encourage attitudes that appreciate health and vitality through eating well and staying active.

The funny thing is, the less you focus on your weight, and the more you focus on just enjoying yourself and doing what fuels you and fulfills you, your weight and body shape will most likely get to where you need them to be.

What I have seen among the tens of thousands of moms in my Stroller Strides program is that those who have lost weight have done so because they have ended up sticking with their program. They have all had different responsibilities, pressures, and obstacles, but somehow they've found a way to make that possible.

For many, it's the social support of exercising with other moms. These moms don't always feel like working out, but they do want to show up and see their friends. And they like how they feel afterward. It's a feel-good experience all the way around. And when the results come because they've been committed to it, it further reinforces their reasons for doing it in the first place and enables them to keep on going.

When it comes to eating well and exercising, the key is to find something you will enjoy. Not only are you likely to integrate it into your lifestyle, you will become the Opti-Mom that your children need. Consider healthy eating an adventure where you are on a journey to try new foods and learn new ways to cook it. You'll be a physically—*and* mentally—strong mom. Kids with parents that are positive role models generally tend to re-create the same behaviors they see.

Remember, it doesn't stop here. You have a lifetime to reinforce the good habits that you've been exposed to from reading this book. By keeping a healthy outlook and practicing healthy behaviors, you'll be a happy, Lean Mommy forever!

RESOURCES

Staying informed is one way to keep yourself inspired and motivated. This chapter gives you an assortment of books, videos, and organizations to help you continue to be active, make healthy eating choices, think body-loving thoughts, and be a great role model as your kids grow. I've even left you with a few of my favorite motivating quotes. For many leads I've simply given you the Web site at the time of publication of this book. If the site has changed when you log on, simply do an Internet search to find the new site.

ABOUT STROLLER STRIDES

Stroller Strides is an organization I developed to help moms who want to make strides in fitness, motherhood, and life. We aim to support new moms in all the aspects of their lives that contribute to their own and their families' well-being. We provide support and instruction on staying active, keeping strong, eating for energy and vitality, and learning to be the best role model mom ever. We give you the strength for motherhood.

How to find a Stroller Strides near you: Log on to www.stroller strides.com or phone 866-FIT-4MOM (866-348-4666).

STROLLER STRIDES® PRODUCTS

STROLLER STRIDES STROLLER

Since 2001, BOB has teamed up with Stroller Strides to bring strolling and fitness together. Now, we are excited to present the Stroller Strides Fitness Stroller. It is BOB's most popular Revolution Stroller with a Stroller Strides Fitness Kit, which includes two exercise tubes of different tensions, a water bottle holder, and the Stroller Strides Fitness Manual to help direct you in your total body workout. It also includes a gift certificate for a week of free classes (if available in your area).

STROLLER STRIDES FITNESS KIT

Turn your stroller time into a total body workout with the Stroller Strides Fitness Kit. You will learn how to use your stroller, the environment, and the exercise tubes that come with this kit for a total body workout. The kit contains two exercise tubes of different tensions, one watter bottle holder, and the Stroller Strides Fitness Manual to help direct you in your total body workout. This console can fit onto most any type of stroller.

STROLLER STRIDES EXERCISE TUBING

You can use this exercise tubing anywhere, anytime. It's lightweight, easy to use, and comes in different intensities.

Go to www.strollerstrides.com to purchase these and other great fitness items.

NEW-MOM RESOURCES

- www.fitpregnancy.com
- www.modernmom.com
- www.parenthood.com
- www.babycenter.com
- www.whattoexpect.com
- *Meditations for New Moms* by Sandra Drescher-Lehman

BREASTFEEDING

- *The Womanly Art of Breastfeeding* by La Leche League
- www.lalecheleague.org
- www.drjacknewman.com
- *The Nursing Mother's Companion* by Kathleen Huggins

NUTRITION

- *Super Baby Food* by Ruth Yaron
- *What to Eat* by Marion Nestle

FITNESS

- *Fit to Deliver,* by Karen Nordahl, Carl Petersen, and Renée M. Jeffreys
- *Exercising Through Your Pregnancy* by James F. Clapp III
- *Cross-Training for Dummies* by Tony Ryan and Martica Heaner

BODY IMAGE/DISORDERED EATING

- *The Body Myth: Adult Women and the Pressure to Be Perfect* by Margo Maine and Joe Kelly
- *Body Image: Understanding Body Dissatisfaction in Men, Women and Children* by Sarah Grogan
- www.bodypositive.com
- www.campaignforrealbeauty.com

POSTPARTUM DEPRESSION

- *This Isn't What I Expected: Overcoming Postpartum Depression* by Karen Kleiman and Valerie D. Raskin
- *Down Came the Rain: My Journey Through Postpartum Depression* by Brooke Shields

EATING ISSUES AND CHILDREN

- *Super Baby Food* by Ruth Yaron
- *Child of Mine: Feeding with Love and Good Sense* by Ellyn Satter
- *Real Kids Come in All Sizes: 10 Essential Lessons to Build Your Child's Body Esteem* by Kathy Kater

OBESITY AND CHILDREN

Food Politics: How the Food Industry Influences Nutrition and Health
     by Marion Nestle
Fast Food Nation: The Dark Side of the All-American Meal by Eric
     Schlosser
SuperSized Kids: How to Rescue Your Child from the Obesity Threat by
     Walt Larimore and Sherri Flynt, with Steve Halliday

PARENTING

- *The Baby Book: Everything You Need to Know About Your Baby
  from Birth to Age Two* by William Sears and Martha Sears
- *Healthy Sleep Habits, Happy Child: A Step-by-Step Program for a
  Good Night's Sleep* by Marc Weissbluth
- *Chicken Soup for the Mother's Soul* by Jack Canfield, Mark Victor
  Hansen, Jennifer Read Hawthorne, and Marci Shimoff
- *The MomsTown Guide to Getting It All: A Life Makeover for Stay-
  at-Home Moms* by Mary Goulet and Heather Reider
- *Mommyhood Diaries: Living the Chaos One Day at a Time* by
  Julie Watson Smith

SOME OF MY FAVORITE QUOTES

I get inspired each day by what I do and the people I interact with.
I love to surround myself with quotes that put life into perspective. Here are a few of my favorites that I hope will also inspire
you . . .

> Benjamin Franklin: "You may delay, but time will not."
> David Viscott: "You must begin to think of yourself as be-
> coming the person you want to be."

Albert Einstein: "There are only two ways to live your life. One is as though nothing is a miracle. The other is as though everything is a miracle."

Dr. Robert Schuller: "What would you attempt to do if you knew you would not fail?"

Dorothy Canfield Fisher: "A mother is not a person to lean on, but a person to make leaning unnecessary."

Jill Churchill: "There is no way to be a perfect mother, and a million ways to be a good one."

INDEX

ABOUT THE AUTHORS

LISA DRUXMAN is the voice for a new generation of moms. A fitness expert, speaker, and author, Lisa is the founder of Stroller Strides®, a unique total fitness program designed for new mothers and their babies. Aimed to support moms in all aspects of their lives, Stroller Strides incorporates both baby and stroller in a one-hour class comprised of a warm-up, power walking, and body toning with the use of exercise bands. Established by Lisa in 2001, Stroller Strides classes are found in more than 300 locations nationwide. Lisa's master's degree in psychology with an emphasis on exercise adherence and weight control has helped her address both the mental and physical aspects of being a mom.

Lisa's outstanding commitment to women and motherhood has led to numerous business awards, and she has been featured on the *Today* show and on CNN, and in *Woman's Day, Redbook,* and *Entrepreneur,* among other publications.

But for Lisa, her greatest achievement is being able to be the best mom she can be first and foremost—and to help other moms do so, too, by basing her entire business around having a career that is supportive of motherhood. Lisa lives in San Diego, California, with her husband, Jason, her two children, Jacob and Rachel, and their beloved dog, Tae Bo.

MARTICA HEANER is the author of several books, including *Cross-Training for Dummies.* She is a health journalist for many national magazines and newspapers, and has a weekly column as the fitness and weight loss expert on health.msn.com. She has a bachelor's degree in English and exercise science from Smith College, and a master's degree in nutrition and a master's in applied physiology from Columbia University. Martica is an award-winning fitness instructor and personal trainer currently based in New York City.